I0414282

[H.A.S.C. No. 114–128]

MILITARY CYBER OPERATIONS

COMMITTEE ON ARMED SERVICES
HOUSE OF REPRESENTATIVES

ONE HUNDRED FOURTEENTH CONGRESS

SECOND SESSION

HEARING HELD
JUNE 22, 2016

U.S. GOVERNMENT PUBLISHING OFFICE

20–795   WASHINGTON : 2017

For sale by the Superintendent of Documents, U.S. Government Publishing Office
Internet: bookstore.gpo.gov   Phone: toll free (866) 512–1800; DC area (202) 512–1800
Fax: (202) 512–2104   Mail: Stop IDCC, Washington, DC 20402–0001

COMMITTEE ON ARMED SERVICES

ONE HUNDRED FOURTEENTH CONGRESS

WILLIAM M. "MAC" THORNBERRY, Texas, *Chairman*

WALTER B. JONES, North Carolina
J. RANDY FORBES, Virginia
JEFF MILLER, Florida
JOE WILSON, South Carolina
FRANK A. LoBIONDO, New Jersey
ROB BISHOP, Utah
MICHAEL R. TURNER, Ohio
JOHN KLINE, Minnesota
MIKE ROGERS, Alabama
TRENT FRANKS, Arizona
BILL SHUSTER, Pennsylvania
K. MICHAEL CONAWAY, Texas
DOUG LAMBORN, Colorado
ROBERT J. WITTMAN, Virginia
DUNCAN HUNTER, California
JOHN FLEMING, Louisiana
MIKE COFFMAN, Colorado
CHRISTOPHER P. GIBSON, New York
VICKY HARTZLER, Missouri
JOSEPH J. HECK, Nevada
AUSTIN SCOTT, Georgia
MO BROOKS, Alabama
RICHARD B. NUGENT, Florida
PAUL COOK, California
JIM BRIDENSTINE, Oklahoma
BRAD R. WENSTRUP, Ohio
JACKIE WALORSKI, Indiana
BRADLEY BYRNE, Alabama
SAM GRAVES, Missouri
RYAN K. ZINKE, Montana
ELISE M. STEFANIK, New York
MARTHA McSALLY, Arizona
STEPHEN KNIGHT, California
THOMAS MacARTHUR, New Jersey
STEVE RUSSELL, Oklahoma

ADAM SMITH, Washington
LORETTA SANCHEZ, California
ROBERT A. BRADY, Pennsylvania
SUSAN A. DAVIS, California
JAMES R. LANGEVIN, Rhode Island
RICK LARSEN, Washington
JIM COOPER, Tennessee
MADELEINE Z. BORDALLO, Guam
JOE COURTNEY, Connecticut
NIKI TSONGAS, Massachusetts
JOHN GARAMENDI, California
HENRY C. "HANK" JOHNSON, JR., Georgia
JACKIE SPEIER, California
JOAQUIN CASTRO, Texas
TAMMY DUCKWORTH, Illinois
SCOTT H. PETERS, California
MARC A. VEASEY, Texas
TULSI GABBARD, Hawaii
TIMOTHY J. WALZ, Minnesota
BETO O'ROURKE, Texas
DONALD NORCROSS, New Jersey
RUBEN GALLEGO, Arizona
MARK TAKAI, Hawaii
GWEN GRAHAM, Florida
BRAD ASHFORD, Nebraska
SETH MOULTON, Massachusetts
PETE AGUILAR, California

ROBERT L. SIMMONS II, *Staff Director*
KEVIN GATES, *Professional Staff Member*
LINDSAY KAVANAUGH, *Professional Staff Member*
NEVE SCHADLER, *Clerk*

CONTENTS

MILITARY CYBER OPERATIONS

HOUSE OF REPRESENTATIVES,
COMMITTEE ON ARMED SERVICES,
Washington, DC, Wednesday, June 22, 2016.

The committee met, pursuant to call, at 10:04 a.m., in room 2118, Rayburn House Office Building, Hon. William M. "Mac" Thornberry (chairman of the committee) presiding.

OPENING STATEMENT OF HON. WILLIAM M. "MAC" THORN-BERRY, A REPRESENTATIVE FROM TEXAS, CHAIRMAN, COMMITTEE ON ARMED SERVICES

The CHAIRMAN. The committee will come to order.

I would like to welcome our witnesses today as the committee examines military cyber operations.

I note that just about exactly 2 months ago President Obama confirmed for the first time that the U.S. is conducting cyber operations against ISIS [Islamic State of Iraq and Syria]. And as the leadership of the Department of Defense [DOD] was discussing this, they said it was the first time that Cyber Command has been given the guidance to go after ISIS. Just like we have an air campaign, we want to have a cyber campaign.

And some of the press went on to discuss that Secretary Carter was pushing for U.S. Cyber Command [CYBERCOM] to have greater freedom to launch attacks and to address tactical cyber threats against ISIS.

I know this committee remains committed to ensuring that the Department of Defense's capabilities to fight and win the country's wars and to be prepared and ready to execute those missions remain on solid footing regardless of which domain we are talking about, including the cyber domain.

The Department has been developing the organizations, capabilities, and personnel needed to operate in cyber since at least 2010. Billions of dollars have been spent. And yet the perception—and you all can disagree with this if you think I am wrong—the perception is the threat is still multiplying faster and growing faster than at least our laws and regulations, policies, rules of engagement are developing.

Still, a fundamental question: What is the role of the military to protect civilian infrastructure in the United States against cyber attack? I do not suggest we are going to get the definitive answer to all of those questions today, but I think that it is important that we discuss not only those but the tactical use of cyber, which the President talked about and which the leadership of the Department has talked about. It is a significant change just in the past few months.

(1)

So we will look forward to hearing from our witnesses about those and other topics, but, first, I would yield to the distinguished ranking member for any comments he would like to make.

STATEMENT OF HON. ADAM SMITH, A REPRESENTATIVE FROM WASHINGTON, RANKING MEMBER, COMMITTEE ON ARMED SERVICES

Mr. SMITH. Thank you, Mr. Chairman. And I agree with your comments about both the complexity and the importance of cyber. And I think the most interesting thing I would like to get out of this hearing is how is the organization coming together, because I think that is the major challenge.

It has been quite a few years now since we have recognized the importance of cyber, and different aspects of our national security apparatus, in addition to the additional different aspects of the Department of Defense, have attempted to address that problem. So we have a lot of people working on it. How coordinated are they? I think that is the great challenge, is making sure that we are getting the most out of the resources that we are putting into this. Because it is a constantly evolving threat, and it threatens every- thing, every aspect. You know, the least little device can be an entry point to a cyber attack. So how do you get a comprehensive look at making sure that you control—or "control" is a bit of an op- timistic statement—have some measure of understanding of where the threats are and how best to address them?

So how the various branches of the military and our broader cyber vulnerabilities—as the chairman mentioned, a lot of those vulnerabilities exist in the private sector. On the defense commit- tee, we have had defense contractors who have been hacked before that have created problems. So how do we comprehensively address this incredibly complex and ever-evolving problem? I think that is the great challenge.

And I will say that I very much approved of what Secretary Carter did, where he had the, you know—I forget what he called it, but where he basically invited hackers to try to find their way in and, you know, learned from that. I think that was one of the best, most cost-effective ways to do it, instead of, you know, doing some contract out to some company and going through a complex process. Just take those people out there who are really good at this and say, "Come at us. Show us our vulnerabilities." I thought that was a very wise way to learn a lot in a cost-effective manner. But, again, the real challenge is having a comprehensive ap- proach to such an ever-evolving and challenging problem, and then, as the chairman mentioned, the legalities of it, in terms of, you know, are our laws and regulations keeping up with it, to make sure that you and the executive branch have the authorities that you need to best protect us and, in some cases, use cyber as an of- fensive weapon where necessary, that those legal questions are also very complicated and ones that we would like to be helpful with if we can.

With that, I will yield back and look forward to the testimony.

The CHAIRMAN. I thank the gentleman.

I also want to mention that, of course, on the front lines for over- sight of this issue, I very much appreciate the Emerging Threats and Capabilities Subcommittee Chairman Wilson, Ranking Member Langevin, who work in this area day to day. I think it is also important, though, for all members to look at these larger cyber issues, which is why we are doing this hearing with the full committee today.

Let me welcome our witnesses: Mr. Thomas Atkin, Acting Assistant Secretary of Defense for Homeland Defense and Global Security; Lieutenant General Kevin McLaughlin, Deputy Commander, U.S. Cyber Command; and Brigadier General Charles Moore, Deputy Director of Global Operations with the Joint Staff.

Without objection, any written material you would like to submit will be included in the record.

Thank you all again for being here.

Mr. Atkin, the floor is yours.

STATEMENT OF THOMAS ATKIN, ACTING ASSISTANT SECRETARY OF DEFENSE FOR HOMELAND DEFENSE AND GLOBAL SECURITY, OFFICE OF THE SECRETARY OF DEFENSE

Mr. ATKIN. Thank you, Chairman Thornberry, Ranking Member Smith, and members of the committee. I am pleased to testify today, along with my colleagues Lieutenant General Kevin McLaughlin and Brigadier General "Tuna" Moore, on the Department's efforts in cyberspace and how we are improving America's cybersecurity posture. It is an honor to represent the Department, and I am proud of the progress we have made in this challenging domain.

The closed hearing this afternoon will go into greater detail on some of the challenges that we face in cyberspace and the Department's efforts to address those challenges, but I wanted to highlight just a few things here this morning.

First, the threat. Today, we face a diverse and persistent threat in cyberspace from state and non-state actors that cannot be defeated through the efforts of any single organization. Our increasingly wired and interconnected world has brought prosperity and economic gain to the United States. However, our dependence on these systems also leaves us vulnerable, and the cyber threats are increasing and evolving, posing greater risk to the network and systems of the Department of Defense and other departments and agencies, our national critical infrastructure, and other U.S. companies and interests.

While DOD maintains and uses robust and unique cyber capabilities to defend our networks and the Nation, that alone is not sufficient. Securing our systems and networks is everyone's responsibility, from the commander down to the individual, and this requires a culture of cybersecurity.

More broadly, preventing cyber attacks of significant consequence against the U.S. homeland requires a whole-of-government and a whole-of-nation approach. To that end, DOD works in close collaboration with other Federal departments, our allies, and the private sector to improve our Nation's cybersecurity posture and to ensure that DOD has the ability to operate in any environment at any time.

Since DOD's cyber strategy was signed in April 2015 by Secretary Carter, the Department has devoted considerable resources to implementing the goals and objectives outlined within the document.

When the Secretary signed the document, he directed the Department to focus its efforts on three primary missions in cyberspace: one, defend the Department of Defense information networks to assure our DOD missions; two, defend the United States against cyber attacks of significant consequence; and, three, provide full-spectrum cyber options to support contingency plans and military operations.

Another key part of our strategy is deterrence. DOD is supporting a comprehensive, whole-of-government cyber deterrence strategy to deter attacks on the U.S. and our interests. This strategy depends on the totality of U.S. actions, to include declaratory policy, overall defensive posture, effective response procedures, indications and warning capabilities, and the resiliency of U.S. networks and systems.

I am proud to say that the Department has made important strides in implementing DOD's cyber strategy since it was signed in April 2015. My colleagues and I look forward to going into greater detail on our strategy and the state of the Cyber Mission Forces as the hearing proceeds, as well as to discuss how our thinking and incorporation of cyber and operations is evolving.

The Department is committed to the security and resiliency of our networks and to defending the U.S. homeland and U.S. interests from attacks of significant consequence that may occur in cyberspace. I look forward to working with this committee and the Congress to ensure that the Department has the necessary capabilities to keep our country safe and our forces strong.

I thank you for your support in these efforts, and I look forward to your questions. Thank you.

[The joint prepared statement of Mr. Atkin, General McLaughlin, and General Moore can be found in the Appendix on page 39.]

The CHAIRMAN. General McLaughlin.

STATEMENT OF LT GEN JAMES K. "KEVIN" McLAUGHLIN, USAF, DEPUTY COMMANDER, U.S. CYBER COMMAND

General MCLAUGHLIN. Chairman Thornberry, Ranking Member Smith, and distinguished members of the committee, I am honored to appear before you today representing the men and women of U.S. Cyber Command. It is my pleasure to do so alongside Assistant Secretary Thomas Atkin and Brigadier General Charles Moore, two gentlemen who keenly recognize the opportunities and challenges the Department faces in the cyber domain.

I would like to focus my opening remarks on U.S. Cyber Command's ongoing efforts to build capability and capacity in the cyber mission force. The cyber mission force [CMF], with unique teams designed to defend DOD information networks, support combatant commander missions, or defend the Nation's critical infrastructure, gives U.S. Cyber Command and the Department a means to apply military capability at scale in cyberspace.

We recognize that success in accomplishing our assigned missions is dependent on three factors: the quality of our people, the effectiveness of their capabilities, and the proficiency that our people bring to bear in employing these capabilities.

U.S. Cyber Command's manpower reflects a true total force effort, encompassing a robust Active Component along with both National Guard and Reserve forces being fully integrated at all echelons, from the highest levels at our headquarters down to our tactical forces that are represented in the cyber mission force.

As of June 10th of this year, out of a target total of 133 teams that will be part of the cyber mission force, we have 46 teams that are at fully operational capable status and 59 that are at initial operating capability status. These teams currently comprise 4,684 total people that we will build to eventually 6,187 when we finish. It is important to note that even teams that are not fully operational are already contributing to our cyberspace efforts as the command operates on a full-time and global basis. The Nation and every combatant commander can now call on cyber mission force teams to bring cyberspace effects in support of their operations. Such work occurs daily, for instance, in the fight against ISIL [Islamic State of Iraq and the Levant], where our teams are conducting cyberspace operations in support of U.S. Central Command's ongoing efforts to degrade, dismantle, and ultimately defeat ISIL.

Training the force to be prepared for its varied missions is imperative. U.S. Cyber Command's annual Cyber Guard exercise, which concluded last Friday, provides realistic training in which Federal, State, industry, and international partners can use their skills against a determined opposition force.

The response to Cyber Guard from our public and private partners has been tremendous. Dozens of critical-infrastructure companies have expressed interest in participating in it. Exercises like Cyber Guard allow senior policymakers to observe the types of issues we see in real cyber attacks and helps us generate a playbook that should save the Federal Government precious time and stress in responding.

In this year's exercise, U.S. Cyber Command expects to certify teams, ensuring they have the requisite training and skills to make an immediate impact in today's fight.

Our command prides itself in being a learning organization. Exercises like Cyber Guard and our other premier exercise, Cyber Flag, which is ongoing at this moment, are key lessons-learned opportunities for us. We also look at everything that we are learning in the growing set of real-world operations and collaboration from the private sector, academia, and partner nations to provide valuable insights to the command and allow our teams to develop and implement new tactics, techniques, and procedures.

Although our people are undoubtedly our most important asset, I would be remiss not to highlight the importance of specialized tools, infrastructure, and capabilities that the cyber mission force needs to execute its missions. Ongoing efforts to develop tools, such as the persistent training environment [PTE], the unified platform, cyber situational awareness, and the Joint Information Environment, must be continued to be resourced. These capabilities are critical in ensuring our cyber warriors are equipped to counter sophisticated and dynamic adversaries.

The accelerated pace of technology, innovation, and our adversaries' changing tactics in cyberspace require well-trained, well-resourced, and an agile force to perform all three of the critical missions we perform in support of the Department and the Nation.

With that, thank you again, Mr. Chairman and members of the committee, for inviting me to appear before you today. I assure you that U.S. Cyber Command is committed to the mission of ensuring the Department of Defense mission assurance, deterring or defeating strategic threats to our interests and infrastructure, and achieving joint force commander objectives. The growing capabilities and capacity of the cyber mission force is adding to our ability to perform this mission.

The U.S. Cyber Command team appreciates the support of this committee that it has shown and looks forward to our continuing partnership with Congress to address the challenges and opportunities in cyberspace. And I am happy to take your questions.

Thank you.

[The joint prepared statement of General McLaughlin, Mr. Atkin, and General Moore can be found in the Appendix on page 39.]

The CHAIRMAN. Thank you.

General Moore.

STATEMENT OF BRIG GEN CHARLES L. MOORE, JR., USAF, DEPUTY DIRECTOR, GLOBAL OPERATIONS (J–9), JOINT STAFF

General MOORE. Thank you, Chairman Thornberry, Ranking Member Smith, and members of the committee. Thank you for the opportunity to speak on behalf of the Joint Staff in regards to the Department of Defense's efforts in the cyber domain.

As all of you are aware, the inherent global nature of cyberspace operations and cyberspace threats causes and creates numerous challenges for the Department of Defense. Additionally, our warfighting capabilities are increasingly reliant on the cyber domain, and it is integral to the advantages we enjoy in everything from our high-tech weapons and communications systems to our ability to rapidly deploy forces around the globe.

Furthermore, trying to keep up with the rate at which technology is advancing in this rapidly changing environment is extremely challenging. It is important to note that, while our adversaries and potential adversaries continue to increase their capabilities, they also share these challenges.

All of that said, the Department of Defense is making significant progress, including the continued build of our cyber mission force, challenging our adversaries' ability to operate freely in cyberspace, and continuing to improve more effectively our ability to defend our networks, information, weapons systems from malicious cyberspace actors.

In regards to building our cyber capabilities, U.S. STRATCOM [Strategic Command] and U.S. CYBERCOM continue to make great strides in standing up our cyber mission forces. These forces are arranged in teams with the objectives to support combatant command requirements, to defend the Nation against cyber attack, and to protect our Department of Defense information networks, information, and weapons systems.

While significant progress in all these areas has been made in the last year, significant challenges do remain, to include equipping the force; establishing a persistent training environment that is responsive to the many layers of required training; recruiting and retaining a professional cyber force; and finalizing the command and control structure for the cyber mission force.

From an operational perspective, CYBERCOM continues to make great progress as we continue to see significant results from our counter-ISIL strategy. In this area, CYBERCOM has not only challenged ISIL, as the President and the Secretary of Defense have publicly stated, but they have also built on our lessons learned to date, establishing a solid foundation upon which to expand the scale and effectiveness of our operations.

From a broader strategic view, our adversaries, who are always looking for something that can provide them an asymmetric advantage, find cyberspace appealing due to the low barriers to entry and the perceived difficulty of attribution. Because of these threats from both state and non-state actors, we work vigorously to harden our networks and weapons systems while educating the total force to create a climate of constant vigilance.

To strengthen the whole-of-government effort to protect U.S. interests, particularly U.S. critical infrastructure, the Department of Defense routinely engages and works with our interagency partners. The Department also regularly engages with our international partners, and there is tremendous interest to expand those cyber relationships.

Finally, as our capabilities continue to grow, we continually engage all of the combatant commands to ensure cyber-enabled effects are being considered for incorporation into their planning processes and to benefit all current and future operations.

While it is well known that we are actively engaged in cyberspace against ISIL, we also recognize that there are other threats in cyberspace that must be planned for and addressed. The Joint Staff is working closely with U.S. CYBERCOM to continue to bring cyber-related options to the table for consideration to support all of our global operations.

As I mentioned, the cyber domain is constantly changing, and we see malicious cyber actors rapidly developing new capabilities at a very high rate. The Joint Staff continues to work closely with CYBERCOM, the combatant commands, OSD [Office of the Secretary of Defense], and our interagency and international partners to secure our networks, our information, weapons systems, and to support combatant command objectives while we defend the Nation against malicious cyberspace activities.

Thank you again for the opportunity to appear today. I look forward to answering any questions that you might have.

[The joint prepared statement of General Moore, Mr. Atkin, and General McLaughlin can be found in the Appendix on page 39.]

The CHAIRMAN. Thank you.

Let me just take a second and remind members that we will have our quarterly cyber update this afternoon at two o'clock in this room. It will be classified, of course, but we will be able to get into greater detail on classified matters at that time.

Mr. Atkin, the Cyber Command achieved full operational capability in October 2010. So we are nearly 6 years down the road. Isn't it time for CYBERCOM to stand on its own as a combatant command?

Mr. ATKIN. I think the short answer to that is yes. We are continuing to look at that within the Department. The Secretary has been evaluating whether to recommend to the President to stand up CYBERCOM as its own unified command. So we are continuing to look at it, but I think we are getting close to a decision and we will be getting something to the President here in the near future.

The CHAIRMAN. Well, we are trying to help you along because section 911 of the defense authorization bill requires that that be done. And I note that Admiral Rogers has testified that becoming a combatant command would allow CYBERCOM to be faster, which would generate better mission outcomes.

I have yet to hear a reason not to do it. And so it seems to me that we shouldn't stew around about this too long, because the goal is better outcomes. And if that is what the result is, we ought to be able to agree and get that done without a lot of delay.

General McLaughlin, let me ask you, we talked about the tactical use of cyber that has been publicly talked about by the President, the Secretary, Deputy Secretary. We obviously cannot get into the details of that in this forum, but what would you say are kind of the broader challenges that have been encountered so far? General Moore mentioned lessons learned. Kind of at an upper policy level, what have we learned so far with what we have been doing against ISIS?

General MCLAUGHLIN. So I think what we have learned is, as we describe to you the cyber mission force that is being built right now, we have learned that the fundamental building blocks of the forces that are actually supporting combatant commands—as we stated in our mission, one major focus is bringing cyber effects to support our combatant commanders. And the war on ISIL is the first at-scale opportunity to do that in support of the U.S. Central Command [CENTCOM].

So the first thing that we have learned is to reinforce that the way we are creating our teams, the expertise within those teams and how they plug into our command and control processes, including to the supported command, is working.

The broader challenges we have is this team is still a young force. As we mentioned, you know, we have quite a few of them that are at initial operating capability, and so, in many cases, this is the first actual live opportunity for these forces to conduct that type of mission. And so the types of lessons we have learned have been a number of just practical lessons about improving the ability for us to do that routinely at scale.

The reason the persistent training environment is so important is to give teams like those that are supporting the war on ISIL, you know, more realistic opportunities to do their work and train in realistic environments prior to actually doing it in combat. So we sort of knew that intuitively, and the actual operations have borne out how important that capability would be.

We have learned how quickly that the Department in general needs to operate from in terms of if there are any policy or anything that needs to be done to support sharing, for example, with partners. And that has happened routinely. So the OSD staff, for example, sits in our twice-a-week update, you know, that we do in this area specifically to want to know is there anything at all that is needed in order to make these operations more effective. We have learned how important that broader team is. Some people might not realize how closely coupled that we are from that perspective.

I think, really, the last is maturity, you know, continuing to do this. We have learned more in the last several months since it has been announced publicly that we are supporting this. It has given us the opportunity to learn and mature, kind of plow back in the lessons learned in a real circumstance that it might have taken us several years to learn some of the things that we are learning, but it is the nature of military operations.

And, in summary, I would just say I think we believe that we are on course, the fundamental tenets of what we are doing are sound, and, you know, our job is to continue to expand capability and capacity against this enemy. And we will talk with you about it and give you some practical examples of that in the closed session later this afternoon.

The CHAIRMAN. General Moore, do you have anything to add on lessons learned or what you see from a Joint Staff perspective?

General MOORE. No, sir. I think most of those that I would add to were touched on by General McLaughlin. I would piggyback on and say the speed of operations and how we can increase the speed of those operations, especially at the operational and tactical level, is something we are very much focused on and is going to be critical to continue to support overall combat operations.

We have also applied the lessons, though, that we have learned from attacks on our own infrastructure and how to better protect ourselves and how better to train our people to defend against that.

The CHAIRMAN. Okay.

Mr. Smith.

Mr. SMITH. Thank you, Mr. Chairman.

Just following up on the raising it to a combatant command level, which we would like to see happen, what are the challenges, what are the steps that you see necessary, Mr. Atkin, to get to that point where you are ready to make that move?

Mr. ATKIN. I think, sir, our biggest challenges are going to be resources, making sure that CYBERCOM has all the right resources as they build out the cyber mission force, as we continue to build out the PTE that General McLaughlin has already mentioned, the unified platform, et cetera, to make sure that they can stand alone and operate as a title 10 military force in support of the combatant commanders. I think that is going to be the key.

Not that we can't do it; it is just a matter of making sure that we are doing it in a sequenced way to make sure that we don't hamper or hurt any operations that we have ongoing and that we continue to gain advantages and do better when we are conducting these operations.

So I don't think there is any one specific thing that is stopping us. It is more about how we make sure it is sequenced to get to the right mission.

Mr. SMITH. And what are the coordination challenges there? Now, there is obviously—we have already coordinated them into a central cyber structure. It just hasn't been given a combatant command status.

As you look throughout DOD, obviously there are a lot of people working on cyber. How do you sort of round all of that up and get it under one unified combatant command? What are the challenges going to be into pulling in those pieces and working with them?

Mr. ATKIN. Well, I think part of the challenge is going to be how we just work internally within the Department. I think we have a good way ahead under the Principal Cyber Adviser, which I am, as well as my role as the Acting Assistant Secretary for Policy. So we work it from both those angles within the Department internally. Under the Joint Staff and as a combatant commander, they work very closely with the other combatant commands to make sure that all the operations are integrated and coordinated.

And then we in policy also work across the interagency and across the intelligence community to make sure the operations are coordinated and the sequence of activities, whether it is the application resources or training or other operations, are coordinated.

Mr. SMITH. What, if any, role does the NSC [National Security Council] play in your cyber operations? This is a subject that has come up in our hearings, you know, the increasing role of the NSC, over the top of, in some cases, the Department of Defense. Are they involved in that? If they are involved, how well do you coordinate and balance what the NSC might be doing on cyber versus what DOD is doing on cyber?

Mr. ATKIN. Well, the NSC is obviously an integral part of the whole-of-government solution and the whole-of-nation solution for any of our activities. And so we keep them advised of the operations that we have ongoing through the interagency process. And we also, when necessary, we coordinate and get the President's permission to conduct operations when his permission is required.

Mr. SMITH. Okay.

Thank you, Mr. Chairman.

The CHAIRMAN. Yeah, we may want to pursue that a little further.

Chairman Wilson.

Mr. WILSON. Thank you, Mr. Chairman.

And thank you, Mr. Chairman, for citing the Emerging Threats and Capabilities Subcommittee. I am very grateful to be chairman of the committee, with extraordinary staff that have worked with everyone here: Pete Villano, Kevin Gates, Katie Sutton, Neve Schadler, and Lindsay Kavanaugh.

And it has also been a remarkable exercise of bipartisanship working with Jim Langevin. And I am particularly grateful, there are subcommittee members here who have been so important. And Elise Stefanik has just been a superstar, coming to every meeting. And I am just so grateful for our other members who are here: Doug Lamborn, Sheriff Rich Nugent, Mo Brooks, Vice Chairman Trent Franks, Duncan Hunter.

But it has just been terrific to work with each of you, it has been so meaningful, on cyber operations, what can be done, but the dangers to the American people. And you are trying to be proactive, and we appreciate that very much.

In fact, General McLaughlin, what are we doing to make better use of coalition forces and capabilities in the planning and execution of our cyberspace operations? How are we aligning our policies, doctrines, and capabilities with our NATO [North Atlantic Treaty Organization] allies?

General MCLAUGHLIN. Mr. Wilson, thank you. And before I answer your question, we also appreciate the great support from the subcommittee and agree that the staff supporting that has been outstanding, and they are very knowledgeable and helpful as we work together.

The ability to integrate our coalition partners into our operations at U.S. Cyber Command is critical. We have broad latitude and authorities that have been granted to us for that partnership. They are actually primarily today within our Five Eyes † partners. We are working and do communicate with NATO, but right now our focus has been our Five Eyes partners, as well as there are some other partners that are really interested in how they actually create the capacity to have their versions of Cyber Command and to do, you know, military cyber operations in countries that are still, I think, at the verge of trying to decide whether they are going to take the same steps that we have taken.

The types of practical areas where we work today with our coalition partners—one, some members of the committee, Congressman Langevin, and the staff were just down at Cyber Guard down at Suffolk last week. And we have Cyber Flag occurring now. We have coalition partners in those sessions, training with our people, learning lessons, creating tactics, techniques, and procedures jointly, and actually practically identifying and overcoming any challenges that limit our ability to work together.

There are key areas where we are doing development of capability together instead of each of us spending the same money to accomplish a certain task. For our close partners, there might be times where we will share a burden or do work like that together. And then, when directed and when authorized, if we have operations where we can actually—we have a partner that can bring a capability or capacity, we are operating with those partners, with shared objectives operationally, and conducting operations in a way that each of our, you know, national capabilities are being used to accomplish objectives that we share.

So I think it is a robust environment right now. It is growing. I think you will see more and more countries want to be part of this partnership. And we will embrace them as they show interest and as they have the capability to partner.

Mr. WILSON. And we have our long-term allies of NATO, but it is exciting, new members such as Bulgaria and Slovakia. I have visited different IT [information technology] centers there, and so, very talented people who will be very helpful.

Additionally, General, how good is the current training exercise and certification process in replicating the real-world challenges using cyber capabilities in tactical operations?

Cyber Command has recently completed a Cyber Guard 16 exercise. Are there any lessons or highlights from that exercise that can be applied to our ability to effectively apply cyber capabilities to tactical operations?

---

† "Five Eyes" refers to a five-nation intelligence alliance involving the United States, United Kingdom, Australia, Canada, and New Zealand.

General MCLAUGHLIN. Sir, that is also a great question. So I would really answer you in two ways.

We have the ability—Cyber Guard is a great example—to do high-fidelity, highly realistic training, where our teams, our tactical forces, can be immersed in a simulated environment that looks real to them and have to perform their duties with an actual opposing force, you know, another group of people that are acting as if they are the enemy. And they have to demonstrate that they have the ability to do their job in that realistic environment. So we can do that, and we are doing it down in the Suffolk area right now.

The issue that we have is we cannot do that at scale. And so we have a program we mentioned in my opening comments, the persistent training environment. That is a focused effort in the Department of Defense to allow us to actually do that type of training routinely, every week, every day, so that the men and women that are on our teams have the ability to do the level of training that we are doing down in Suffolk right now. We only do that a few times a year. So our job is to do that consistently, all the time, like we do in every other domain.

Mr. WILSON. My time is up. Thank you.

Thank you, sir.

The CHAIRMAN. Mr. Langevin.

Mr. LANGEVIN. Thank you, Mr. Chairman.

And, first of all, Chairman, I want to thank you for your support and your interest in cyber, as you have continued on when you were chairman of the Emerging Threats and Capabilities Subcommittee. And I appreciate the work that you are doing now at the full committee level, along with the ranking member, Mr. Smith. And I agree with my chairman on the subcommittee now, Mr. Wilson, that it has been an exercise in bipartisanship, and deeply appreciate the work of the staff.

Secretary Atkin, I want to thank you for your testimony today, along with you, General McLaughlin and General Moore. Thank you for what you are doing on cyber and, again, being here today. General McLaughlin and General Moore, as we have discussed this morning, the Cyber Guard homeland defense training exercise just concluded. I was very pleased to be able to attend that exer- cise. I very much enjoyed being able to witness the exercise take place in person. I was very impressed with what I saw. And I wanted to thank you all for being such great hosts for that exercise.

Chairman Wilson had asked—not surprisingly, we are on the same page. I wanted to know what your takeaways were from the exercise at the highest levels. So anything else you want to elaborate on lessons learned from the exercise, feel free.

But I also would like to know beyond that what lessons have been learned with respect to the cyber mission forces executing operations in a geographic combatant commander's area of responsibility as they pertain to each mission. And are roles and responsibilities of involved entities being refined and solidified, as well as command and control of CMF?

General MCLAUGHLIN. Congressman, let me just take both of your questions.

I think we, on the first question about high-level lessons learned that we have seen coming out of this year's Cyber Guard, while the full report will be written in the next few weeks, we do have some initial, you know, I think, broad insights that come from it.

One is an increasing understanding of how many of the other partners—you know, so that, as you mentioned, that is a whole-of-government and international exercise that simulates some attack of significant consequence that occurred, you know, outside of the DOD networks. What has really been interesting and our lesson is how many players both within our government, within industry, and within—and I mean broadly, beyond DOD, within our government—and our coalition partners are coming to this exercise.

It continues to grow, because it is an opportunity to tease out not only practical, technical ways for our teams to defend and respond, but those complex challenges about how different parts of the Federal Government coordinate in response and how does that work; how do we work with industry, and you know better than most the complex issues associated with government forces actually connecting with industry cyber terrain and how we should do that most appropriately and most effectively; and then how we do that at scale with our partners.

So that continues to be a key lesson for us, is the scale of people that want to participate. And every time we think we have reached the outer limits of who ought to be there, we realize there are more players that can or ought to come.

And then the last thing is just to really reinforce the question, I think, from Mr. Wilson—that is, the need to be able to train at the level—the men and women that are down at Cyber Guard are asking us, you know, we really would like to have this capability routinely. This is great training. It is the best—most of them say it is the best they have ever had. And our goal is to let them do the best all the time.

I think your question regarding what have we learned in terms of how—in our mission of supporting combatant commanders, are there broad lessons that we have learned and are we adapting and being innovative: When we built the cyber mission force and our initial command and control models, we just started with what we thought would work. And what has been very interesting and, I think, a positive step is the Department, often led by General Moore's team down on the Joint Staff, has continued to lead and ask how do we refine and change and adapt our command and control processes.

And we have made a number of adjustments in the last 18 months. We will talk this afternoon. We have made changes in how we command and control and focus our forces just in the counter-ISIL operations. So we really are learning and changing a lot. There is no one saying, "That is the way we have always done it," because the way we have always done it has only been about, you know, 2 or 3 years. So we are changing as we need to.

The one thing I think is a key just tenet that all of us need to understand—and we are seeing this play out in the support to CENTCOM—cyber capabilities aren't just there to solve cyber problems. There are adversaries that present themselves in a variety of ways that we could hold at risk. They might have a cyber capability that I will use some other tool or capability to counter, and they may have a non-cyber capability that we are going to use a cyber tool to counter.

So that is one thing that I think the whole Department is learning, is that you don't pigeonhole cyber capabilities against cyber problems, is that we integrate broadly with CENTCOM, we integrate broadly with combatant commands, and we bring what is unique that we can offer to their mission, as opposed to defining problems only as cyber-only. And I think that has been a key lesson for everybody, and I think it is a powerful one for the Department.

Mr. LANGEVIN. Thank you, General. Thank you and your team for the work you are doing. And I was very impressed, like I said, with what I saw at the Cyber Guard exercise. And I agree that training, training, training has got to be a key part of us doing this going forward and seeing that persistent training environment be maximized and supported in a very robust way.

So thank you, Mr. Chairman. I yield back.

The CHAIRMAN. Thank you.

Mr. Lamborn.

Mr. LAMBORN. Thank you, Mr. Chairman.

Thank you all for your service to our country in various capacities.

And I am going to build off of what Representative Langevin was just asking. This month, in a press interview, NATO Secretary General Jens Stoltenberg said that a major cyber attack could trigger a collective response by NATO, including a response using conventional weapons.

Now, I know that is NATO, not the homeland. But, in this fast-evolving field, what can you tell us, what are you in a position to state publicly are the evolving rules of engagement where something would trigger a cyber response from us or a kinetic response from us?

Mr. ATKIN. Sir, as I have said before, you know, it is a whole-of-government response, so a cyber attack would not necessarily mean we have to have a cyber response back to that. And each of those actions would be evaluated on a case-by-case basis by the en- tire interagency and the government.

So we would look at any cyber attack, whether it is against a combatant commander overseas or here in the homeland, on a case-by-case basis and determine what the significance of it was. And then we would use a whole-of-government approach, whether it is a diplomatic means, economic means, law enforcement, or military action, to respond to that.

Mr. LAMBORN. Okay.

Anything to add to that, Generals?

General MCLAUGHLIN. Well, sir, I will say for our mission, as General Moore mentioned, our job one is defending the DOD information network. That is ongoing 24 hours a day, 7 days a week. We have all the authorities that we need today and are growing the forces, so any threat that manifests itself—and, you know, these are short of attacks, you know, formal attacks or wars, but they occur all the time. And so the authorities we need within that domain, which is our main defensive mission set, we have those authorities. And we spend a great deal of our time day to day managing and responding to a breadth of those activities.

In our closed session later today, we will give you some insights into the scale, just the daily size and scope of what that looks like, and then a specific example of an operation that we have conducted recently against a very specific threat so you can see that, you know, a little more fully.

Mr. LAMBORN. Okay. Well, thank you. That is reassuring to me, and I am sure it is reassuring to everyone who might be listening.

And changing gears, before my time is up, in Israel they are doing more with collaborating with the private sector and consolidating everything that they are doing into one location for synergy.

What do you see as the possibility or the future of collaborating with the private sector here in the U.S., with places like Silicon Valley, Seattle, et cetera, to harness the public-sector creativity and expertise in this area? What do you see as the future of that?

Mr. ATKIN. Sir, I would say, in that regard, the future is here. We are integrated in with the private sector, I think, well. And we are going to continue to grow that, whether it is through the Defense Innovation Unit Experimental [DIUx] out in Silicon Valley that Secretary Carter stood up, how we leverage the skills that the National Guard and Reserve forces bring from their private-sector jobs and we leverage those skills as integrating those folks into the cyber mission force, or continuing to work with the private sector in response to cyber attacks through exercises such as Cyber Guard.

So we are already working with the private sector pretty well, I think. We are going to get better at that. And we are leveraging the skills of the National Guard and Reserve folks as part of the cyber mission force.

Mr. LAMBORN. But you don't see anything in the works like what Israel did, for instance, where there would be an actual consolidation into one location? That is a much smaller country, obviously.

Mr. ATKIN. I would say that I don't see that, no, sir. I think we have good coordination and collaboration through the Department of Homeland Security [DHS], the FBI [Federal Bureau of Investigation], Department of Justice, as well as the other sector-specific agencies—Commerce, Treasury, et cetera—with their sectors. But I don't see us consolidating all those activities into one location.

Mr. LAMBORN. Okay.

Thank you so much, Mr. Chairman. I yield back.

The CHAIRMAN. Ms. Gabbard.

Ms. GABBARD. Thank you, Mr. Chairman.

Gentlemen, good morning.

I would like to ask you about defense support to civil authorities, in particular, I think, the vulnerabilities and the concern about some type of domestic cyber attack on critical infrastructure that would threaten public safety.

So I am wondering if you can talk about that but also specifically answer whether or not the DOD and the National Guard would assist in responding to that type of attack, as well as, you know, what actions are being taken to eliminate those vulnerabilities and to make it so these types of attacks are not possible.

Mr. ATKIN. That is a great question and a great challenge for our country, is how we protect our critical infrastructure.

We work very, very closely with the Department of Homeland Security, who is primarily interacting with the critical infrastructure and have that responsibility, to not only provide them with information regarding threats but to help define how we respond as a nation to an attack on the critical infrastructure.

Where DOD gets involved is an attack of significant consequence. We have the responsibility to defend against an attack of significant consequence.

Ms. GABBARD. How do you define "significant consequence"?

Mr. ATKIN. That would be determined by whether loss of life, physical damage, economic impact, or how it might impact our foreign policy. So those are some of the factors that we would evaluate of an attack of significant consequence.

But I was——

Ms. GABBARD. Could I just ask a follow-up to that?

Mr. ATKIN. Yes, ma'am.

Ms. GABBARD. As you define loss of life, if there was an attack on an electrical grid, caused a major power outage, hospitals no longer able to care for people, and loss of life in that respect, would that fall under that definition?

Mr. ATKIN. I would have to say I am not sure I could answer a hypothetical like that. I think that the factors of the impact would certainly be evaluated and determined.

What I would say is, regardless of whether it is an attack of significant consequence or not, the Department of Homeland Security would respond. And if they needed assistance from the Department of Defense, they would ask for that assistance, and we would respond with assistance through the Department of Homeland Security to help that critical infrastructure. Part of that occurred during Cyber Guard, where we exercised that capability. A request for assistance from the Department, and we responded.

So the other piece of that is the National Guard, and they have cyber mission capability. They are being trained to the same capability as the rest of the title 10 force. And they can respond under their own State authorities. We recently completed the coordinate, train, advise, and assist policy guidance within the Department to allow National Guard troops to use Department of Defense resources to respond to a cyber event under State authority. And we are continuing to work other policies.

I just recently set up a meeting to work with all the different combatant commands, NORTHCOM [Northern Command], PACOM [Pacific Command], Cyber Command, Joint Staff, and our Office of General Counsel to determine exactly how we are going to set up our defense support of civil authorities more holistically. The policy has been in process for a period of time, and I want to make sure we have senior leadership attention on it very directly.

Ms. GABBARD. Thank you. I think this is something that, obviously, we are going to have to continue to discuss and understanding the differences of whether a state or non-state actor were to come and launch a traditional type of military attack on critical infrastructure versus a cyber attack, how the DOD is involved or not in those situations. You know, given the types of attacks that we are already seeing from both state and non-state actors in the cyber world, you know, having clearly defined roles and responsibilities between DOD and DHS, I think, is critically important.

Thank you.

The CHAIRMAN. I agree.

Ms. Stefanik.

Ms. STEFANIK. Thank you, Mr. Chairman.

And thank you to the witnesses for testifying today and for your leadership on this issue.

I want to focus my questions for the full panel on the evolution of the cyber threat and how we maintain the edge on a 21st-century battlefield.

The news, as you know, this past year has been filled with stories about the evolving strategic threats in the cyber realm from near-peer adversaries like Russia and destabilizing threats from both state and non-state actors within the Middle East. Just this week, I read an article that CNN reported that ISIS has been able to collect information on 77 U.S. and NATO Air Force facilities around the world.

In March, at a hearing on this subject, I asked Admiral Rogers how confident he was moving forward that our cyber capabilities are robust enough to face the threats of the future on multiple fronts.

Can you speak specifically to your concerns about adversarial cyber capabilities and your assessment of our own capabilities in comparison moving forward?

And then the second part of my question is: Given the unique challenge of prosecuting simultaneous cyber threats from multiple adversaries, where do you feel the cyber community is assuming risk for readiness?

General MCLAUGHLIN. So, ma'am, within this area—and I can address that and would also be glad to get into the specifics on the threat side when we are in the closed session. But, broadly, you stated it correctly. The threat today is diverse. It certainly is represented not only by large nation-states that are very, very capable, to organizations like ISIL or criminal or hacker organizations. The barrier to entry is not that high, and the ability to innovate and use technology to continue to evolve is actually there.

On the Cyber Command side, I think the key thing that we think is important is focused on people and technology. I will do technology first.

The ability to have the tools and the capability and sort of an integrated suite, a defense-in-depth approach across our whole enterprise, we think, is proving to be very effective. And the ability to bring new technology—that is one of the reasons the connection to Silicon Valley and other places is so important, is we don't field something, like a cyber capability, that we will use for a decade or a few decades. You know, we want the latest capability, and as soon as it is not the latest, we would like to have the next set of technology.

So those tools and capabilities that are throughout the depth of our network are critical.

The most important part, though, are our people. We have talked about the persistent training environment, but we haven't really talked about even the foundational training that goes into the cyber mission force.

And some people ask why does it take a few years to take an initial accession and get them to that level, is that we are training all of our people to a very, very high standard, a joint standard across the force. Because, in our view, it is in the minds of our people that are going to allow them to keep up technologically with what the threat is doing.

We are not just training our folks to operate equipment. We are training them to understand the domain, the foundational technologies, the advanced technologies. And, in some cases, they are adapting the technology that they have right there at their fingertips in real time to counter our adversary or to develop tools to do that.

So I think the most important part for us to stay ahead is making sure that we invest in the people and that they have those types of skills.

Ms. STEFANIK. And on the multiple-fronts portion of the question, given the fact that there are multiple cyber threats, whether you consider a near-peer adversary like Russia or non-state actors in the Middle East, where do you feel the cyber community is assuming risk to readiness?

General MCLAUGHLIN. Well, I think the way I am going to answer your first question is thinking broadly, assuming risk to military force readiness broadly. Cyber is a thread through everything that we do—our platforms, our networks, our own critical infrastructure within DOD. And we can't defend everything all the time at the same level.

And so the way that we have approached that, and, to some degree, broadly with the Department—this is not a decision Cyber Command on its own makes. But we are given a set of priorities of the most important combat and military capabilities that need to be hardened and defended and where mission assurance is most critical if they were to be attacked, across a broad front.

And so we don't think about doing that against one threat. We sort of prioritize the most important things against the most important threats. And those are the things we think have to be defended at the highest level. And we would accept risk if there was an area that was either not as important or something we felt was lower down the priority, because you just can't defend all of it to 100 percent all the time.

Ms. STEFANIK. Thank you.

Would the other witnesses like to add anything?

Mr. ATKIN. On the risk measurement, I would say that we evaluate the critical infrastructure that is required for the Department, using our mission assurance strategy and our cyber strategy combined, to identify those most critical elements of the infrastructure that we need to protect, and then we evaluate and prioritize those pieces.

And we are not only protecting them from physical damage, but now we are also mapping out the key cyber terrain to understand where the most critical vulnerabilities are.

Ms. STEFANIK. Thank you. My time has expired.

The CHAIRMAN. Mr. Ashford.

Mr. ASHFORD. Thank you, Mr. Chairman.

I would also like to second the comments regarding Chairman Wilson and Ranking Member Langevin for their leadership on Emerging Threats. It has been a very interesting year and a half. I have two topics I would like to cover. One is deterrence in the cyber world and then, secondarily, the Information Technology Ex- change Program and how you see that evolving. I probably could start with General McLaughlin on deterrence.

When we are dealing with what the public generally thinks about in the deterrence area, we are talking about nuclear weap- ons. In this case, we are dealing with cyber. We know to a certain extent how many nuclear weapons are out there. We can identify specifically the threat. And we have decades of experience in deal- ing with deterrence as it relates to nuclear weapons and other mat- ters regarding deterrence.

In cyber, where we have 80,000 or so attacks a year, it is hard to identify where they are coming from and who has the capabili- ties at any given time. It is very dynamic, and you have talked about that. Could you just kind of define for me what deterrence means in the cyber world and how that is evolving?

Or Mr. Atkin.

Mr. ATKIN. I will go ahead and jump on that a little bit.

So, from a cyber perspective, as we have mentioned before, a cyber attack doesn't always mean a cyber response. Attribution is key. And that is probably the greatest challenge in any cyber at- tack, is attributing it to either a state actor or a non-state actor. We look at it as we want to make sure that, from a deterrence policy, it is declaratory, that everybody understands exactly where we stand and that we are able to impose cost.

So the first part of any deterrence policy and our deterrence pol- icy is denial. We want to make sure we deny the adversary the op- portunity to achieve the effects they are trying to achieve, and that is by developing and having good cybersecurity.

The next piece we want to be able to do is have a very resilient system. And so we want to build the systems to be resilient. And if they are attacked, as General McLaughlin has already said, we can't protect everything all the time, but if they are attacked, that they will be able to be recovered and be resilient and back on line again, denying the adversary the goals they are trying to achieve. And then the third step of our deterrence policy is to impose cost. And that cost, whether it is diplomatic, law enforcement, economic sanctions, or military actions, to include cyber response, those are part of the deterrence policy that we would use to respond or to sig- nal to a state or a non-state actor.

Mr. ASHFORD. General.

General MCLAUGHLIN. Sir, just in accordance with the direction we received from OSD, even in the—Mr. Atkin mentioned the Sec- retary signed our new DOD cyber strategy. Within that was direc- tion for us to actually take steps to meet those three goals.

And our primary effort has really been all the defensive activity, the work we do to make our networks more resilient and to make it to where an adversary couldn't achieve their goals that they might try to achieve by attacking our cyber infrastructure. Many people don't think deterrence involves that, but it has really been the anchor of what we are doing, that we have been ordered to do and we are accomplishing within Cyber Command.

The imposed-cost piece as just part of that force we have is aimed at bringing options to bear that would be there for the Secretary and the President, if that was directed.

Mr. ASHFORD. Thank you.

Could I just ask a question about the Information Technology Exchange Program? I believe in the NDAA [National Defense Authorization Act] we expanded that program a bit and added more slots.

Is that program—so take, for example, the Sony case, where there were issues in the Sony technology that made it easier or less difficult to attack the Sony technology, whether it is the silos of their various businesses within Sony or whatever it is. So there are issues in the private sector that are different from in the DOD sec- tor and Federal sector. And they are diverse, and it depends on the industry, and it depends on what they do.

So is the purpose of the Information Technology Exchange Program to help to put in place people into the private sector directly to help them to deal with those threats?

And then, vice versa, if there is somebody in the private—as I understand it, this is what this is. So if in the private sector we have someone who is really exemplary or proficient in a particular aspect of cybersecurity, that we can bring those people in on a temporary basis to address those issues that we see. Is that essentially what we are doing here?

Mr. Atkin.

Mr. ATKIN. Sir, I will have to take that one for the record. I am not as familiar with that program.

[The information referred to can be found in the Appendix on page 57.]

Mr. ASHFORD. But, okay, aside from that program then, are there other strategies that are in place to allow us to bring experts in the private sector into the military on a temporary basis and vice versa? Is that part of what we are doing? Maybe I misunderstood the program.

Mr. ATKIN. I am not—as far as actually bringing someone from the private sector into being a member of the military, I am not familiar with that program at this time. I know that the Secretary has talked about that as part of the force of the future, some of the changes. So I know that is something that he is beginning to talk about as we move forward.

What I would say is that we try to leverage the skills from the private sector through our National Guard and Reserve forces, as we mentioned earlier, and leverage those skills that they gain in the private sector. And we also do things like the bug bounty, where we actually have hackers come in and take a look at our DOD systems and see if they can hack those systems.

So there are different ways we are trying to leverage the private sector and the skills that the private sector has to improve our own cybersecurity.

Mr. ASHFORD. Thank you.

General.

General MOORE. Sir, if you are referring to the Cybersecurity Information Sharing Act—I think that is what you are referring to——

Mr. ASHFORD. Right.

General MOORE [continuing]. That the Congress recently passed, that has gone a long way towards helping the Federal Government share threat information with industry and vice versa.

The two main benefits of that act are that it, first off, reduces the risk of any legal liability to any of those industry partners that we have when they share that information, and also decreases any economic or business advantage that might be gained through the act of sharing that type of information. So it is really knocking down a lot of those barriers.

Mr. ASHFORD. Thank you, Mr. Chairman.

The CHAIRMAN. Mr. Rogers.

Mr. ROGERS. Thank you, Mr. Chairman.

This will be a question for all of you. Do any of you believe that the Department of Defense should use equipment provided by Huawei or ZTE, each of whom have links to Chinese military and intelligence apparatus, and each of whom have links to sales, illegal sales to Iran, in violation of U.S. sanctions?

Mr. ATKIN. Sir, I am not as familiar with those technologies. Certainly, we would want to take those factors that you just highlighted into consideration, if we were going to use anything like that, and those would probably be—the risk would have to be evaluated based on those threats on whether we would use those technologies.

Mr. ROGERS. So you are not familiar with either of those two Chinese providers?

Mr. ATKIN. I have heard of them, but I am not a technical expert to make a good decision.

Mr. ROGERS. General McLaughlin.

General MCLAUGHLIN. So, sir, I would just say, so I haven't heard of the first company that you mentioned, but what I would say broadly is all the equipment that we use or field as part of our DOD mission, you know, it is heritage, and the supply chain associated with that is something that is important that we assess. Based on the utility of that equipment, we assess, you know, what vendors are appropriate and which ones shouldn't be.

So I am not prepared to tell you, because I just don't know what exclusions might be there for both of those companies broadly across the DOD. But I do know for our core capabilities, it is something that before we buy it, we buy that capability, its security and that our knowledge of its supply chain go into the factors before we make a broader procurement.

Mr. ROGERS. General.

General MOORE. Sir, I am really just piggybacking on what the two other gentlemen have said. Supply chain vulnerabilities are absolutely real and they should be considered anytime we are looking at any equipment that we might purchase on behalf of the DOD or the Federal Government.

Mr. ROGERS. That was with relation to DOD, you are saying. What about a U.S. cleared contractor? Do you apply a different

standard to them? What would you advise them if they were thinking about using equipment from one of those two Chinese firms? Mr.

ATKIN. Sir, I am not—again, I am not on the acquisition side, and I
know that we work very closely on the acquisition side with the
different contractors through the defense industrial base and to
ensure that their systems are secure. So we are always looking at
the supply chain vulnerabilities and the risk. And so our advice to
any of the contractors that support the Department of Defense or
any of the interagency, I think we would recommend them to take a
hard look at their supply chain vulnerabilities and to ensure that
their information is secure and their operations are secure.

Mr. ROGERS. So I guess I am hearing from you all that you don't
have a list of Chinese firms that you are concerned about right
now, or you have a list, but you are not familiar with it?

Mr. ATKIN. Sir, I am not familiar with a list.

Mr. ROGERS. Do you know if you have a list?

Mr. ATKIN. I do not, no, sir. And we can take that for the record.

[The information referred to can be found in the Appendix on
page 57.]

Mr. ROGERS. Yeah. General McLaughlin, do you know if you all
have a list of Chinese firms you are concerned about having access
to your supply chain?

General MCLAUGHLIN. Sir, I don't. I just—because it is all han-
dled within our acquisition chain of command—you know, the folks
that actually procure our equipment, which is outside what we do
at U.S. Cyber Command.

Mr. ROGERS. If you could do what Mr. Atkin just said, take it for
the record and let me know back, I would appreciate that.

Thank you, Mr. Chairman. I yield back.

[The information referred to can be found in the Appendix on
page 57.]

The CHAIRMAN. Ms. McSally.

Ms. MCSALLY. Thank you, Mr. Chairman.

Thank you, gentlemen. I am not sure if you answered this. Sorry.
I was at a Homeland Security classified briefing. But I do want to
ask about the Secretary of Defense announced we were doing cyber
operations against ISIS just starting a few months ago. The caliph-
ate was declared 2 years ago. I know probably the details would
be more in a classified realm, but this is a very important domain,
and this terrorist organization is using cyber in a way that we have
never seen other terrorist organizations use before.

What took so long and what was the decision-making process
that is having almost 2 years go by before even thinking about
fighting in this domain?

Mr. ATKIN. Ma'am, that is a great question. I think the bottom
line is that we probably started more than 2 months ago. I don't
have the exact date and time that we began to conduct cyber operations against ISIS. We continue to respond to ISIS and their—
both the use of the social media, the sharing of PII [personally
identifiable information] about military service members and their
families. And so it wasn't always necessarily a cyber response to
ISIS, but it certainly was a response to their cyber activities.

Ms. MCSALLY. So I know there is always this tension, I mean,
I was in the military, between keeping comms [communications] up

and running so that we can collect on it versus taking it out so they can't communicate. But, you know, we have known cells in Raqqa that are directing training, that are directing operations very specifically, you know, targeting against Americans' way of life.

Why isn't the Internet shut down in Raqqa? Like, why did we not have cyber operations 2 years ago going against their command and control as part of our centers of gravity and using all elements of military power to take them down?

Mr. ATKIN. Yeah. And I know they will get a little bit more into this in the closed hearing later today, but the fact is we were going after their command and control systems. We may not have been using necessarily cyber activities to do that. There always is a balance between collecting information and shutting it down.

And certainly, going after specific nodes to hamper and stop the use of the Internet by ISIS is important, but we also have to respect the privileges and rights of citizens to have access to the Internet as a whole and as a country. So it is a careful balance, even in Raqqa or Mosul or anywhere, on how we balance the rights to have access to the Internet versus the use of the Internet illegally by folks like ISIL.

Ms. MCSALLY. Yeah. I would like to follow up for sure in the classified setting with a little more details.

The second question is we were dealing with this, my last assignment was at Africa Command, just trying to deal with the functional commands and the geographic commands. Can somebody speak to, I don't know, General McLaughlin, how the relationship is working and is there duplication of cyber capabilities at the geographic commands? And how does that work if you are conducting operations and the coordination with the geographic commands?

General MCLAUGHLIN. Yes, ma'am. I think it is working pretty well and I don't see any duplication right now. And when we—later, we will give you some great details with regard to U.S. Central Command, but generally, each of those combatant commands has a cyber element within it that is at their headquarters level, and their job really is sort of understanding broadly what their command is trying to achieve in the domain. We have the forces that are actually, you know, both the defensive and offensive forces that they are using. And so the practical way that it is working today, for example, you know, in real world operations is we have, you know, daily, you know, whether it is targeting meetings or planning sessions where the supported commander and our staffs and our teams are interacting routinely.

Our job is to support them, and, you know, we deliver the effects, you know, on the targets they need at the time they need, but we bring the capability.

Ms. MCSALLY. Okay. Thanks. My last question is about the laws of armed conflict and some of the challenges that we have had in this domain in identifying what is an armed attack and, you know, what constitutes the ability to be able to respond and Article 5 and all that kind of stuff. So can there—can we just have some comment on where we are on that and whether there is still some further definition that needs to happen related to the clear authorities that are needed to be able to operate in this domain?

Mr. ATKIN. I would say specifically to your question what defines an act of war, I think is what your question is regarding cyber acts, that has not been defined. We are still working towards that definition across the interagency.

As far as an attack of significant consequence, which the DOD would respond to, in the homeland, we don't necessarily have a clear definition that says this will always meet it, but we do evaluate it based on loss of life, physical property, economic impact, and our foreign policy. So there are some clear lines in the road which we would evaluate any specific cyber act or incident and how we would respond to that.

Ms. MCSALLY. Okay. Great. My time has expired.

Thank you.

The CHAIRMAN. Let me follow up on just a couple things.

Mr. Atkin, I understand the concept of proportionality as you are looking for any sort of military effects. But are you arguing that the citizens of Raqqa have some sort of inherent right to access the Internet that you all have to try to weigh?

Mr. ATKIN. What I am trying to explain is that I think that when we start talking about taking out the Internet, there are always challenges to how you do that and where you do it in space. So the Internet service providers who provide that Internet service to a region are much broader, generally, than just the adversary's single command and control node. And so how that effect occurs has greater impact than just against the adversary, and we have to weigh that in when we make all our decisions. And whether that is a kinetic or a cyber operation, those factors are always weighed in and the impact to the civilian populace.

The CHAIRMAN. Okay. Well, I think I understand the concept of proportionality, as I say, throughout warfare. I just got concerned there for a second that there was some sort of inherent right to be on the Internet that was a factor in you all's decision making.

I want to go back. I think both the generals mentioned the importance of speed of decision making. Mr. Smith asked earlier about NSC and when you have got to keep them informed and when you have got to get permission. There has been a fair amount written about the air campaign, and I had quoted Secretary Work earlier who said, just like we have an air campaign, I want to have a cyber campaign.

Some of the things that have been written about the air campaign are that for some sorts of—so we have got airplanes circling above Iraq or Syria. For some sort of attacks, then a certain level of command can make a decision, say it is okay to drop your bomb. Others have to go up to the CENTCOM, others have to go up to the Secretary of Defense, some have to go to the President. Meanwhile, the planes, they are circling. And that one of the challenges to being more effective against ISIS is this multilayered decision-making process, which has slowed down or hindered the ability of our military to be as effective as they could be. Now, that is with bombs, an air campaign.

I am concerned, I guess, that we are developing the same sort of multilayered bureaucracy decision-making process when it comes to cyber. And part of the challenge with the air campaign is by the time you get permission to do it, the target is gone. And I have personally talked to pilots that have had that happen. Now, when things are moving at the speed of light, if we go through this multi-layered decision process to push the button on a cyber response, then we are going to be hopelessly behind.

So, I guess, if anybody can address where we are with this speed of bureaucracy matching the speed of the world that would reassure me, I would like to hear it.

Mr. ATKIN. Yes, sir. What I would say is in the area of hostilities, CYBERCOM has the authorities by which to operate and conduct cyber effects and make that decision at the CYBERCOM level. So they certainly have those authorities to do that. And I think they can talk more in greater detail in the closed session this afternoon on the specific authorities that they do have.

The CHAIRMAN. Okay. Well, we will talk more about it. But, again, just drawing the analogy to the air campaign, I am not yet reassured.

Mr. Atkin, I want to follow up Mr. Lamborn's question about the NATO announcement last week. Does that NATO announcement indicate NATO has agreed that a cyber attack can trigger Article 5?

Mr. ATKIN. That is my understanding.

The CHAIRMAN. And so then the question for the NATO nations is going to be at what level of cyber attack would trigger Article 5, because there are at least media reports of a fair amount of constant cyber activity in some of the Baltic and Eastern European countries coming from the east.

Mr. ATKIN. As far as I know, there has not been a determination made or a decision made on what would constitute a cyber attack that would trigger Article 5, so I would have to take that one for the record.

[The information referred to can be found in the Appendix on page 57.]

The CHAIRMAN. Okay. And, finally, the questions that Ms. Gabbard was asking about defense of civil authorities and attack of significant consequence, is one of the factors which would be considered in determining whether it is an attack of significant consequence who the actor is, whether it is a state actor or not?

Mr. ATKIN. That could be a factor, but I wouldn't say it is one of the primary factors. The primary factors are loss of life, economic impact, how it may impact our foreign policy, and then physical property. So those are the four primary factors that we would evaluate from an attack of significant consequence, whether that is a state or non-state actor.

The CHAIRMAN. I guess the questions that come to my mind relate to, say, terrorism information we get. We may get information that a terrorist attack is in the works. We don't know exactly what the target will be, we don't know exactly what the consequence will be. And if you have to wait to see what the consequence is, then it is going to be too late, right?

Mr. ATKIN. Yes, sir. I would also say it is similar to a cyber threat. If you have an unknown—you have a known—I guess I will back up.

If you have the potential for a cyber attack, but you don't know where it is coming from, you don't know who is going to do it, you certainly would alert people to provide them an opportunity to maybe heighten their security, just like we do in the physical world with a terrorist threat where we are not sure exactly the when or where it will happen. I would say very——

So it is similar, but we can't necessarily—if we don't know where it is coming from and who is going to do it and how it's going to happen, it is very hard to go in and then stop that from happening.

The CHAIRMAN. Yeah. Well, I understand. And I realize you don't want to get into hypotheticals. My concern is we know where it is coming from. Country X, Y, Z that has tremendous cyber capability is preparing to do something, and the question is whether we wait and let them do it or try to at least take defensive action to man- age the consequence of it. And to me, that is where this gets very difficult.

I understand, you know, if we know it is going to have significant loss of life, yeah, that is pretty easy. But if we see—and I guess I would say the difference is we know ISIS is going to do whatever they can get away with, so they are going to use their full capa- bility to kill as many people as they possibly can. We don't know that about some state actors who have tremendous cyber capa- bility. And so waiting to see how much of their capability they will use and how that fits into this standard of attacks of significant consequence seems, to me, to be somewhat problematic.

Mr. ATKIN. Well, sir, I think we are maybe talking past each other a little bit. One is how we respond to an attack and when we respond under defense support of civil authorities versus mak- ing sure we have a good cybersecurity posture to make sure that we are defended prior to an attack. So certainly, there is—we would not necessarily evaluate the potential before it happens. We would go ahead and provide defensive measures through DHS, with DHS to help prevent an attack, and then we evaluate after an attack happens.

The CHAIRMAN. Yeah. I realize these terms get a—okay. So we are going to wait back and defend, but we are not going to take action to prevent the attack to begin with. And then so the defini- tion of offense and defense in this situation gets a little tricky. And I am not trying to pin you down. I am just——

Mr. ATKIN. No, no. I——

The CHAIRMAN [continuing]. Trying to explore some of the com- plexities of these challenges.

Mr. ATKIN. Certainly, a known threat coming from a known actor that we know is coming after the United States, I would say that we would certainly evaluate that. And those decisions would be made by the Secretary and the President on what kind of actions we would take to stop that from happening, and that would be on a case-by-case basis.

The CHAIRMAN. Yeah. Okay.

Mr. Langevin.

Mr. LANGEVIN. Thank you, Mr. Chairman. Again, thank you to all of our witnesses here.

I just want to go back to the training environment again. Gen- eral McLaughlin, the House Armed Services Committee, as you know, fully funded the persistent training environment initiative, and I understand other committees did not provide full funding. So my question is, can you describe the persistent threat training environment and the impact of proposed cuts? And what stage is the concept in? Has it been fully approved by the Joint Staff?

General MOORE. Sir, if it is okay, I will attempt to answer that question for you.

Mr. LANGEVIN. Sure.

General MOORE. So as was indicated earlier, persistent training environment gives us a couple of things that we don't currently have, like on the Joint Information Operation Ranges. We don't have the scale of the complexity to truly represent a realistic and relevant threat, the ones that we are truly trying to train to. So that is the big advantage that it gives us, and, of course, as the name indicates, it is permanent.

Right now, the initial capabilities document is under review, it should be signed within the next 1 to 2 weeks. And if that happens and the funding stays in line, we expect to have an IOC [initial operating capability] by fiscal year 2019.

Mr. LANGEVIN. Very good. Thank you.

I know we have talked about this on some point, but General McLaughlin and General Moore, what role does the Cyber Threat Intelligence Integration Center, established in 2015, play in support of cyber operational planning?

General MCLAUGHLIN. Sir, in terms of cyber operational planning, on our day-to-day operations at U.S. Cyber Command, it is not playing a role in the planning side. It is mostly playing a role of collecting, you know, integrating intelligence and information on what the threat is doing and then at times, you know, providing information back out to all the rest of the government operation centers. But they are not playing any operational planning role in support of U.S. Cyber Command missions today.

Mr. LANGEVIN. Very good. Thank you.

And, General McLaughlin, let me ask you, what lessons have been learned about the construct of the cyber mission force over the last year? Is the force manned, trained, and equipped, and postured correctly to address threats in their respective mission areas?

General MCLAUGHLIN. Sir, I believe we have learned that it is manned and equipped properly and postured to respond. Some areas that we have learned, we think, in this space, agility is really important. And we have found and in many cases we have task organized sub-elements of teams. We will—each of those teams is comprised of specific sets of skills. And we have learned that it is very effective to take sub-elements of certain teams and task organize them against a specific problem set or a threat and leverage, you know, smaller, more agile elements of those teams, whether they be defensive or offensive teams, to provide you a more immediate and a more tailored mission capability.

And so we initially didn't think about it that way, but we have some very innovative commanders that use that approach. We do that in other domains of warfare. We task organize, and it works really well in the cyber mission force. It is one example of what we have learned of a way we would employ it. The basic building blocks, we think, are sound, but at times how we might sort of tactically organize it for a specific dynamic problem, that task organization has proven to be a great agile way for us to think about how we employ it.

Mr. LANGEVIN. Very good. And going back to the concept area of the Cyber Guard exercise that we just had. If we have a large-scale cyber attack that leads to infrastructure damage and DOD is called in to assist, what organization within DOD will take the lead? And in this scenario, what will NORTHCOM's role be, and how is DOD getting ready to assist after such an attack?

Mr. ATKIN. So NORTHCOM would, obviously in the case of a defense support to civil authority, they would have command and control responsibility. CYBERCOM would be in support of that. The force that would be responsible to respond would be determined on what the specific request was from the interagency. So it could be road clearing, it could be helping transport something from one location to another, which would be a TRANSCOM [Transportation Command] responsibility, road clearing was the Army Corps of Engineers. And if it is a cyber response where we need to help from a cyber perspective, it would be CYBERCOM.

Mr. LANGEVIN. Very good. Thank you.

Could we—well, before my time is about to expire, in terms of, for the record, building out the training environment, what is still needed and how can we be of assistance further?

General MCLAUGHLIN. So, sir, right now, the main thing that is needed is the broad four elements of that persistent training environment. We have some parts of it, but the—we have one part, it is called the event management side of it, is where we actually plan all the training events that would need to occur globally, assess the performance of each of the players that are being evaluated, where our aggressor force would reside. It is really all the things that make it training. That is one of the key things that the fiscal year 2017 budget request is the first real year of commitment to that funding, is building the technical capability to manage all of that capacity.

And so what you saw last week was really a manual way of doing that, not at scale. And so what we are trying to build is the foundational technical capability to do that routinely at scale and to have the people there that actually provide that training. And that is what we want to get started on really seriously in fiscal year 2017.

Mr. LANGEVIN. Well, we look forward to continue supporting you in that effort, General, as you build that out. As for me, it was time well spent going to see that exercise, and I encourage others to do the same. So thank you.

And with that, I yield back.

The CHAIRMAN. Mrs. Walorski.

Mrs. WALORSKI. Thank you, Mr. Chairman.

And I just wanted to follow up, Mr. Atkin, on a question from Mr. Rogers' line of questioning about China. I understand that you are not involved with the acquisition side of the business, but from a cybersecurity perspective, how concerned are you about counterfeit parts entering into our systems, and how can we best defend those threats?

Mr. ATKIN. As mentioned, we constantly and consistently look at our cyber chain vulnerabilities and evaluate, working with our defense industrial base partners and other contractors that provide resources for the Department, on different vulnerabilities and how we would stop those vulnerabilities, to make sure that the only equipment that comes into the supply chain is free of counterfeit or high-risk material.

Mrs. WALORSKI. Thank you.

And, General McLaughlin, I want to direct this question to you, but I want to just give you a really quick background. I represent the great State of Indiana, where we have Muscatatuck Urban Training Center. This remarkable training facility includes its own fully functional power plant. At this training center, rotational units are able to participate in a number of real scenarios, but one of the most compelling is where the power grid there is hacked or taken offline in the exercise. As I consider the devastating consequences associated with that kind of attack to our grid, I am interested if the Department has the training resources necessary to adequately prepare for one of these scenarios.

So to you, sir, you described the Cyber Guard and Cyber Flag exercises in your remarks earlier. Are you confident in your ability to fully stress your forces in a way that prepares them to respond and defend against any sort of contingency scenario? And then, what are the gaps, the significant gaps in training, if there are any?

General MCLAUGHLIN. So, ma'am, I would say today we are—I wouldn't be able to say that I am confident that we are able to respond to all of those. You listed a broad range of potential contingencies.

The reason the persistent training environment is so important, you just—in fact, I would love to learn more about the capability you just described in Indiana. But part of that persistent training environment is being able to replicate each of those unique classes of terrain. Industrial control systems are different than platforms like airplanes and tanks, and they are different than just networks. So part of what we will build are the high-fidelity replications of each of those unique types of targets that we would need to defend against.

We are building the ability for civil or other partners to bring their own range emulations and connect into that environment, and then the people that want to actually do it, have the place to sit down, plug into what looks to them to be their realistic replication of what they are trying to defend, and then do their job in a realistic scenario against hackers or, you know, attackers that are trying to do it.

So today, I would say we don't have the capacity at scale to cover that range. We have a concept. That is why we are proceeding with our program to actually do that. And it has the flexibility to accept the ability for other partners, non-DOD partners, to plug into that environment and do training. We are doing it manually today at Cyber Guard, and I think you will see us do that more at scale with more partners than just, you know, U.S. DOD participants.

Mrs. WALORSKI. I would like to invite you, General, to come into Muscatatuck in Indiana. I would love to share additional information with you about their capability and having those resources there with that fully functioning power plant, what they have been able to learn, the kind of activities they are running, and what it does, I think, for training for all of our forces. So I would love to extend an invitation to you to come there and see it for yourself.

General McLAUGHLIN. Yes, ma'am. Absolutely. Thank you.

Mrs. WALORSKI. Thank you.

I yield back, Mr. Chairman.

The CHAIRMAN. Mr. Johnson.

Mr. JOHNSON. Thank you, Mr. Chairman.

And, gentlemen, thank you for being here today to discuss what is really a turning point in our approach to offensive and defensive military policy.

Being a member of the Judiciary Committee, specifically the IP [Intellectual Property] Subcommittee, cyber and tech issues are at the forefront of my mind, and I am encouraged to see that we are taking necessary steps to ensure that the U.S. maintains a comparative and competitive advantage in this arena.

Mr. Atkin, with respect to—well, I will ask this question first, because it is related to the previous question that my colleague, Mrs. Walorski, asked.

With respect to the coordination with civil authorities, specifically at the State and municipal level, and in consideration of the fact that U.S. Army Cyber Command is moving to Fort Gordon, I have heard concerns about how this may put neighboring communities at risk. For example, if Fort Gordon is hit with a cyber attack, is it independent enough from the local energy grid, that it does not down power to the entire region, affecting hospitals, schools, et cetera? And what can we do in Congress to help facilitate coordination with local authorities in the event that such an attack happens?

Mr. ATKIN. Sir, for——

Mr. JOHNSON. And I am sorry. I meant to ask that question of General McLaughlin.

General McLAUGHLIN. So, sir, I am not aware right now of any element of the move that you just—you mentioned a concern potentially with U.S. Army Cyber Command moving to Fort Gordon. The scenario you described is not one that has been brought to my attention, so I am not aware of any direct connection of that move to an increased threat or risk to the local community.

We do step back and look broadly at the risk to all of our military installations. Many of them for their critical power and infrastructure are using, you know, commercially provided control systems for, you know, electricity, water, and power. But we haven't really seen any analysis that shows the location of military installations is driving a higher likelihood that an attack against them would have some unique impact on the local community.

So I am not saying that it wouldn't, I am just not aware of any analysis.

Mr. JOHNSON. Well, I have heard concerns about it from State and local officials, and I think it is an area that reassurance is due, at the very least. So in terms of coordinating with State and local leaders, I think that that would be something important for you to consider. And I thank you for that answer.

Mr. Atkin, with respect to the development of cyber-related technology, much has been said of the need for DOD to attract brilliant hacker minds from the private sector. How can we in Congress help improve the DOD's ability to attract tech startups who are leading the way in cutting-edge technology?

Mr. ATKIN. Thank you, sir, for that question. I would say the first stop would be, which is something that you have already provided, which is excepted service opportunities for the civilian sector or the civilian personnel in the Department involved in cyber activities. I would say the broader we can make this excepted service across the entire cyber enterprise, that would be very helpful. So broadening out the excepted service for civilian employees would be helpful to be able to bring in those really smart hackers and other people that have a cyber background.

Mr. JOHNSON. I have even heard some suggestions about creating startup incubators within specific government agencies. Do you see that as something that can be coordinated within DOD?

Mr. ATKIN. Sir, I am not familiar with the incubator model. I know that we reach out through our Defense Innovation Unit Experimental out on the West Coast and how we work with Silicon Valley and others. I know that we leverage the skill sets of our Reserve and National Guard force to make sure that we—those are the young, smart minds that are working in the private sector and bringing expertise back into the Department through their Reserve and National Guard status. So I know we are going that route, but I am not as familiar with the incubator model that you describe. Mr.

JOHNSON. Either one of you, General Moore or General McLaughlin, care to comment about that?

General MOORE. One of the brother systems, if you will, or programs to the DIUx that Secretary Atkin mentioned is the In-Q-Tel model, which was actually started at the CIA [Central Intelligence Agency] organization, overt. Right now, there is about eight governmental agencies or organizations that go through the In-Q-Tel model specifically out in Silicon Valley. And you can think of it more of as a venture capitalist type of organization, where we bring problems that we want innovative and quick, hopefully, solutions to.

That money is taken by the In-Q-Tel organization and invested in many times these startup organizations that have innovative technologies. And we have started that program at the Department of Defense to help us solve another specific problem, and I see that program continuing to grow. It has showed a lot of promise.

Mr. JOHNSON. Thank you.

Mr. ATKIN. One other—our Defense Digital Service recently ran a bug bounty using a hacker program basically to contract out for hackers to come in and take a look at DOD systems and to see if they could hack into it. So that was another model by which we did reach out to the private sector and leverage the skill sets they have to improve our own cybersecurity.

Mr. JOHNSON. Thank you. And thank you for your service to the Nation.

And with that, I yield back.

The CHAIRMAN. Chairman Wilson.

Mr. WILSON. Thank you, Mr. Chairman. As we conclude, I think it is quite appropriate that Kevin Gates of the Emerging Threats Subcommittee is seated with the chairman. I really appreciate,

Kevin has an almost 20-year history of working on these issues, before many of us had ever heard of them.

So, Chairman Thornberry, we are just fortunate to have such great people who are assisting our country protecting American families.

General Moore, what legal or policy framework governs information conflict of the sort evolving from the use of social media for propaganda and recruitment? As a tactical matter, how successful are efforts to counteract the use of social media?

General MOORE. Yes, sir. So as I think you are keenly aware, a lot of what we are doing to counter ISIL in Iraq and Syria revolves around using cyber as a conduit for military information support operations, or MISO/PSYOP [psychological] operations, to specifically get after those types of problems. We have the authorities to conduct those types of operations, and I don't see any limitations at this time.

Mr. WILSON. And indeed, sadly, we saw with the San Bernardino mass murder, with the Orlando mass murder, there was a direct social media contact and availability that has resulted in mass murder across our country.

Secretary Atkin, I was grateful, in a deterrence policy you mentioned multiple responses that are possible. And that can't be more important than right now because we have had so many incidents of cyber attacks just in the last month. The Democratic National Committee came under cyber attack, there were North Korean attackers of smartphones of South Korean officials, there were power outages affecting tens of thousands of people in western Ukraine; over and over again, just incidents that are incredible.

And then one that got my attention at the very time that the dangerous Iranian nuclear deal was being put together. In November 2015, Iran's Revolutionary Guard hacked the email and social media accounts of a number of Obama administration officials in an attack. Was there any response to that attack?

Mr. ATKIN. I am not familiar exactly with the event and what our exact response was of all those situations that you describe, but what I would say is when we are able to have attribution, that we would respond at a time and manner and place of our choosing.

Mr. WILSON. Well, it is so obvious it was in such bad faith, the Iranian Revolutionary Guard would, at a time of negotiations or implementation, show such bad faith as to attack the Obama administration that was placing such faith in them. But we certainly want to be working with you, and there just has to be multiple responses that make sense.

And I want to thank you all for being here. And I yield back the balance of my time.

The CHAIRMAN. Mr. Atkin, Mr. Wilson prompts me to try one more question. Okay. The primary job of CYBERCOM is to defend DOD networks. But in thinking about defense support to civil authorities, if there is a foreign country that launches some sort of cyber espionage or cyber attack against a server, a private server by the Secretary of State, or looking for information about a leading candidate for President, is that an attack of significant consequence? It is not against DOD networks, but it goes to either government officials or someone who is wanting to be a government official.

Mr. ATKIN. Yes, sir. So we would evaluate each attack, if we were evaluating based on whether it was an attack of significant consequence on the loss of life, property, damage, economic impact, and foreign policy. So I would say we would evaluate each of those attacks based on that factor on whether and how we would respond.

The CHAIRMAN. Seems to me it is pretty tricky when you start into political campaigns, say somebody is the nominee for President, if there are further sorts of espionage.

I was just about to adjourn, and Mr. Franks walks in. Do you have a question?

Mr. FRANKS. Mr. Chairman, I do, but I will be brief, sir.

The CHAIRMAN. The gentleman is recognized.

Mr. FRANKS. And I appreciate your forbearance, to say the least. I didn't mean to come in and—you know, sometimes people, when they walk in, end the party. That is usually the situation for me. General McLaughlin, I will be really brief here. In an open set-ting, the best you can, how is Cyber Command being employed to fight against the Islamic State?

General MCLAUGHLIN. So, sir, you know, in this setting, and, again, we will get into more detail with you in the closed session, our organization and the teams, the tactical forces that are within U.S. Cyber Command, a subset of those have been allocated and directed to support operations against the Islamic State. We are operating in support of U.S. Central Command. It is, you know, a focused activity that is recurring and is a major element of what the command is focused on day to day. We have leaders within our organization who, you know, subordinate leaders to Admiral Rogers, that it is their only job. And we are bringing—every capability that we have in this area that are available to us, we are making available to that fight.

Mr. FRANKS. Are there any restrictions that might be called rules of engagement or anything like that on how the command might be employed against the Islamic State, any restrictions?

General MCLAUGHLIN. Well, sir, a bit earlier, one thing Mr. Atkin described is within the area where we are actually conducting these operations, we have adequate authorities, the authorities we need to operate. Our operations in cyberspace are subject to the same, you know, rules of every operation. So we are constrained by the law of armed conflict and other limitations, but they are really not any different for what we are doing as in any other domain. So within the operation, we feel like we have the authorities and the flexibility we need to support that particular operation.

Mr. FRANKS. One last question, Mr. Chairman.

We know a little about the cyber doctrine and military structure of adversaries like Russia, China, and others. What is our understanding of those things related to actors like Syria, Iran, Israel, or Germany?

General MCLAUGHLIN. Well, sir, I would just say, you know, in this setting, what we know about the cyber aspirations of our potential adversaries, all I would say is we know that most of them have realized this is a tool available to them, you know, as an instrument of power, and it is a tool they can use without a significant amount of investment, and they can have a relatively small number of people, or buy expertise.

Our coalition partners, those countries that we partner with, we are partnering with each of them as they—and many of them are on their own looking at building military cyber capability, and we partner with them closely. They visit, they are looking for advice from DOD and the United States. And to the degree they want to come see this, we routinely meet with them and talk with them about how we could help them, you know, be part of a broader group that can defend themselves and operate together in cyberspace.

Mr. FRANKS. Well, thank you.

Mr. Chairman, I yield back my minute and 54 seconds. Thank you, sir.

The CHAIRMAN. I thank the gentleman.

Thank you all for being here and for answering our questions. We will look forward to seeing you a little bit later today.

The hearing stands adjourned.

[Whereupon, at 11:52 a.m., the committee was adjourned.]

APPENDIX

June 22, 2016

PREPARED STATEMENTS SUBMITTED FOR THE RECORD

JUNE 22, 2016

STATEMENT OF

MR. THOMAS ATKIN

ACTING ASSISTANT SECRETARY OF DEFENSE FOR

HOMELAND DEFENSE AND GLOBAL SECURITY

OFFICE OF THE SECRETARY OF DEFENSE;

LIEUTENANT GENERAL JAMES K. MCLAUGHLIN

DEPUTY COMMANDER, U.S. CYBER COMMAND;

AND BRIGADIER GENERAL CHARLES L. MOORE JR.

DEPUTY DIRECTOR GLOBAL OPERATIONS (J-39), JOINT STAFF

BEFORE THE

HOUSE ARMED SERVICES COMMITTEE

22 JUNE 2016

INTRODUCTION

Chairman Thornberry, Ranking Member Smith, and Members of the Committee, thank you for inviting us to discuss the Department of Defense (DoD) efforts in cyberspace. It is an honor to appear before you today and we appreciate the opportunity to explain the progress the Department is making to improve America's cybersecurity posture.

We plan to focus our testimony on the approach the Department has taken in implementing DoD's Cyber Strategy and how our approach to this mission space is advancing. Additionally, we will discuss our efforts to continue to develop, train, and equip our Cyber Mission Force (CMF). Finally, while we cannot discuss the particulars in this setting, we will also highlight how cyber capabilities support military operations within the context of Operation INHERENT RESOLVE. The Islamic State of Iraq and the Levant (ISIL) represents a serious and complex threat, and continues to use the internet to intimidate its enemies, recruit fighters, incite violence, and conduct or inspire attacks. Protecting the territory and people of the United States remains DoD's highest priority, and cyber operations are one component in support of the whole-of-government effort against ISIL.

THE CYBER THREAT LANDSCAPE

In addition to the threat posed by ISIL, we continue to face a diverse and persistent set of threats from state and non-state actors who probe and scan DoD networks for vulnerabilities. While the United States has benefited greatly from the increasingly wired and interconnected global landscape, cyber threats are increasing and evolving, posing greater risks to the networks and systems of the Department of Defense and other federal departments and agencies, our national critical infrastructure, and U.S. companies and interests.

As the recent indictment of Iranian cyber actors who infiltrated a hydroelectric dam in New York and launched attacks against the U.S. financial sector between late 2011 and mid-2013, as well as the attack on Sony Pictures Entertainment in 2014, demonstrates, the cyber threats to the United States and its infrastructure are real. If malicious cyber actors gain access to DoD networks, they can potentially manipulate information or software, destroy data, harm computers that host data, and even impair the functioning of systems that computers control. The successful intrusion into the Joint Staff's unclassified network demonstrates that despite our efforts, sophisticated actors can penetrate DoD systems. More broadly, the cyber incident involving Ukraine's power grid that led to power outages and damage to electrical control systems illustrates the broader impacts on society that cyberattacks can have. While DoD maintains and uses robust and unique cyber capabilities to defend our networks and the nation, often these measures alone are not sufficient. Securing systems and networks is everyone's responsibility – from the commander down to the individual and across the Federal Government – and requires a culture of cybersecurity.

Interagency discussions focus heavily on criminal activity in cyberspace, but nations in many ways still represent the gravest threats because of the skill and resources they can bring to bear. The states that we watch most closely in cyberspace remain Russia, China, Iran, and North Korea. Russia and China are both very capable cyber operators, while Iran and North Korea represent lesser, but still significant, challenges to U.S. interests. At DoD, we remain vigilant, and devote substantial resources and effort preparing for future threats that could be directed against the U.S. homeland, critical infrastructure that the Department relies on, and communication networks that we require to operate during a contingency.

DOD STRATEGY AND MISSIONS

Since DoD's Cyber Strategy was signed in April 2015, the Department has devoted considerable resources to implementing the goals and objectives outlined within the document. When Secretary Carter signed the Strategy, he directed the Department to focus its efforts on three primary missions in cyberspace: (1) defend DoD information networks to assure DoD missions, (2) defend the United States against cyberattacks of significant consequence, and (3) provide full-spectrum cyber options to support contingency plans and military operations.

In addition to DoD's core missions in cyberspace, one of the Department's key policy goals in cyberspace is to deter cyberattacks. DoD is supporting a comprehensive, whole-of-government cyber deterrence strategy to deter attacks on U.S. interests. This strategy will depend on the totality of U.S. actions, to include declaratory policy, overall defensive posture, effective response procedures, indications and warning capabilities, and the resiliency of U.S. networks and systems.

Fundamentally, however, deterrence is largely a function of perception, and DoD has three specific roles to play within a whole-of-government deterrence strategy. First, we seek to deny the adversary the ability to achieve the objectives of a cyberattack, so our adversary will believe any attack will be futile. We do this through strengthening our cyber defenses and reducing our attack surface. Second, we want to improve our resilience, so our adversary will perceive that even if any single attack is successful, we can reconstitute quickly so that their ultimate objective will not be achieved. The Department is already training to operate in a "cyber contested environment," to demonstrate that we can continue our mission even while under cyberattack. Lastly, for deterrence to be effective, the adversary must believe that our ability to respond to an attack will result in unacceptable costs imposed on them. Costs may be imposed through a variety of mechanisms, including economic sanctions, diplomacy, law enforcement, and military action. Our task at the Department is to plan and prepare to conduct Title 10 military operations, including through cyberspace, to impose costs on the adversary.

PROTECTING OUR NETWORKS

Our primary mission remains the defense of the Department's information systems to assure the ability to conduct DoD missions; if these systems do not function, our national military power is at risk in all of the domains in which it operates. The Department's recent budget submission clearly reflects the high priority of this effort. Of the $6.8 billion of DoD's cyberspace budget request, $3.9 billion are designated for cyber security or cyber defense activities. This contributes to a broader $19 billion investment across the Administration on cybersecurity and in support of the Cybersecurity National Action Plan.

In order to secure its networks, the Department is pursuing multiple lines of effort to include the DoD Cybersecurity Discipline Plan and the DoD Cybersecurity Scorecard. These two initiatives mutually reinforce one another and ensure that cybersecurity becomes "commanders business" and receives direct leadership focus to address shortcomings and gaps. The Cybersecurity Discipline Plan focuses on strong authentication, device hardening, reducing the attack surface, and alignment to cybersecurity and computer network defense providers; the Scorecard measures the most important elements of the DoD Cybersecurity Discipline Plan. The data from the Scorecard is reviewed by the Secretary. Also, in March 2016, Secretary Carter launched the first cyber bug bounty program in the history of the federal government, "Hack the Pentagon," to reward vetted hackers who report bugs related to vulnerabilities or hacking exploits. This innovative initiative tested the Department's networks and engaged the hacker community to contribute to the security of the internet.

At the Command level, USCYBERCOM is working to harden and defend our networks. In addition to the DoD Chief Information Officer (CIO), who provides the technical standards and implementation of policy, USCYBERCOM works daily with the National Security Agency (NSA), the Defense Information Systems Agency (DISA), the Combatant Commands, and the military services to secure, operate, and defend DoD systems. Improving our collective cyber defenses is a whole-of-government and whole-of-nation endeavor that also requires close partnership with our allies.

THE CYBER MISSION FORCE

The complete build of the Cyber Mission Force underpins DoD's primary missions in cyberspace and all our efforts in this domain. The heart of DoD's cyber capability – both offensive and defensive – lies with a dedicated professional cyber force. USCYBERCOM manpower reflects a true total force effort encompassing a robust active component along with both Guard and Reserve forces fully integrated at all echelons from USCYBERCOM headquarters to the tactical edge of our CMF.

Recruiting and retaining a talented cyber workforce is a top priority for Secretary Carter. Section 1107 of the Fiscal Year (FY) 2016 National Defense Authorization Act (NDAA) granted DoD the authority to establish a Title 10 Civilian Cyber Excepted Service Workforce to assist in carrying out the responsibilities of USCYBERCOM and the elements of the Military Departments supporting it. This step from Congress was an important and welcome step forward to manage our civilian cyber workforce, and will provide them the fulfilling career path and competitive pay that we need to keep our best employees.

Our Combat Mission Teams (CMTs) are on the cutting edge and operate with the combatant commands to support their missions, while National Mission Teams (NMTs) prepare to defend the nation's critical infrastructure from malicious cyber activity. Cyber Protection Teams (CPTs) defend DoD Information Networks alongside DoD Computer Network Defense Service Providers. The Department continues to build out DoD's 133 CMF teams, and the Services are actively working to support the achievement of full operational capability for the entire CMF by the end of FY18. We have also begun to transition from focusing on "building the force" to monitoring more traditional "readiness" metrics, with all the CMF teams reporting their readiness within DoD reporting systems, like our warfighting units do.

The Cyber Mission Force gives USCYBERCOM the capacity to operate on a global scale. The National Command Authority can call on CMF teams to bring cyberspace effects in support of global military operations. Such work occurs daily, for instance, in the fight against ISIL, as Secretary Carter has discussed. Portions of the CMF are executing cyber operations to make it more difficult for ISIL to plan or conduct attacks against Americans and our allies. Cyber is a domain like air, sea, and land, and as we continue to conduct cyber operations in support of broader operations, like we are doing against ISIL, we expect to talk about it with increasing openness.

USCYBERCOM recently employed CPTs to respond to intrusions in DoD systems. CPTs played an important role in remediating the Joint Staff's unclassified systems after an intrusion last year, and in correcting the misconfiguration the intruders had utilized.

Training the force for such missions is imperative. DoD regularly participates in exercises that explore and push to improve policies and processes for providing assistance to DoD components as well as civil authorities in the context of a cyberattack. In these exercises, such as the Department of Energy's GridEx and ClearPath series, and USCYBERCOM's CYBER GUARD Exercise, which took place last week, DoD works with a wide range of interagency, state, local, and industry participants to understand and improve planning for scenarios to provide emergency assistance cooperatively with DHS, the FBI and the Sector-Specific Agencies identified in Presidential Policy Directive 21. These exercises have helped inform DoD's thinking regarding what kind of support we might be asked to provide and have also been an important tool for educating industry about what the federal government, including DoD, might provide in a crisis. The support for CYBER GUARD from our public and private partners has been positive. Exercises like CYBER GUARD allow senior policymakers to observe the types of issues seen in real cyberattacks, and helps us generate lessons learned that should save the federal government precious time and effort in crafting its response.

In addition to exercises, the Department continues to advance its thinking and organization on the topic of cyber test and training ranges. The primary purpose of cyber test capabilities and ranges is to enable the development, acquisition, and sustainment of DoD resilient systems, while training ranges are critical to mission rehearsal and sustainment of DoD's Cyber Mission Forces. The FY 2015 NDAA, Section 1633, directed that DoD establish Executive Agents for a Cyber Training Range and a Cyber Test and Evaluation Range. This legislation was instrumental in helping the Department establish roles and responsibilities in the area of training for the CMF – critical to the readiness of our forces - and in NDAA FY 2016, this work was leveraged to support the designation of the Executive Agent for Section 1645,

Persistent Training Environment (PTE). PTE is critical to the collective training of the CMF and budget cuts to this training capability place the readiness of our forces at serious risk.

CONCLUSION

The Department is committed to the security and resiliency of our networks and to defending the U.S. homeland and interests from attacks of significant consequence that may occur in cyberspace. We have undertaken comprehensive efforts, both unilaterally and in concert with our interagency partners, allies, and the private sector to improve our nation's cybersecurity posture and to ensure that DoD has the ability to operate in any environment at any time. Our relationship with Congress is absolutely critical to everything the Department is doing. To that end, I am grateful for the committee's interest in these issues, and I look forward to your questions.

Thomas Atkin
Acting Assistant Secretary of Defense for Homeland Defense and Global Security

Tom Atkin is the Acting Assistant Secretary of Defense for Homeland Defense and Global Security. He is responsible for advising the Secretary of Defense and Under Secretary of Defense for Policy on policy, strategy, and implementation guidance across a diverse portfolio of national and global security issues. These issues include countering weapons of mass destruction, cyber operations, homeland defense activities, antiterrorism, continuity of government and mission assurance, defense support to civil authorities and space-related matters.

Previously, from November 2014 to August 2015, Mr. Atkin served as Principal Deputy Assistant Secretary of Defense for Homeland Defense and Global Security. Prior to his appointment in 2014, Mr. Atkin was a Director for Raytheon U.S. Business Development for Homeland Security. In this capacity he was responsible for linking technological, engineering and service solutions to maritime, border, public safety and other security-related requirements in the homeland security market. Mr. Atkin also served as the Managing Principal of The Atkin Group, a management consulting firm that provided broad strategic and operational counsel on intelligence, maritime security, crisis management, incident response, and interagency coordination to senior government and corporate officials.

Mr. Atkin retired from the Coast Guard as a Rear Admiral (Upper Half) in June 2012 after more than 30 years of service in various operational and strategic roles. He has significant experience across the whole of government and has served in support of the White House National Security Staff, Department of Defense, Department of Homeland Security, Federal Emergency Management Agency (FEMA), U.S. Coast Guard, and U.S. Navy. His senior leadership positions included serving as Assistant Commandant for Intelligence and Criminal Investigations; acting Assistant Commandant for Marine Safety, Security and Stewardship; Special Assistant to the President and Senior Director for Transborder Security on the White House National Security Staff; Commander of the Coast Guard Deployable Operations Group; Deputy Principal Federal Official to the FEMA Gulf Coast Joint Field Office; and Chief of Staff to the Principal Federal Official for Hurricanes Katrina and Rita. His previous Pentagon assignments were Chief, Maritime Homeland Security and Defense Policy, Office of the Secretary of Defense, Homeland Defense; and Chief, Counter-Terrorism Branch, Chief of Naval Operations (Deep Blue).

He is a graduate from the United States Coast Guard Academy with a Bachelor of Science in Mathematical Sciences, and holds a Master of Science in Management Science from the University of Miami.

Lt Gen James K. "Kevin" McLaughlin
Deputy Commander, U.S. Cyber Command

Lt Gen James K. "Kevin" McLaughlin is the Deputy Commander, U.S. Cyber Command (USCC), Fort Meade, Maryland. USCC directs the forces and daily activities of U.S. Cyber Command and coordinates the Department of Defense computer network attack and computer network defense missions.

General McLaughlin entered the Air Force in 1983 as a graduate of the U.S. Air Force Academy. He has commanded at the squadron, group, wing and numbered air force levels and has served on the staffs at major command headquarters, combatant command headquarters, the National Reconnaissance Office, Air Force headquarters, and the Office of the Secretary of Defense. Prior to assuming his current position, General McLaughlin was the Commander, 24th Air Force and Commander, Air Forces Cyber, Joint Base San Antonio - Lackland, Texas.

EDUCATION
1983 Bachelor of Science degree in general studies, U.S. Air Force Academy, Colorado Springs, Colo.
1986 Squadron Officer School, Maxwell AFB, Ala.
1987 Master's degree in space systems management, Webster University
1995 U.S. Army Command and General Staff College, Fort Leavenworth, Kan.
2000 Air War College, by correspondence
2002 National Defense Fellowship, Center for Strategic and International Studies, Washington, D.C.
2006 Joint Professional Military Education Phase II, Joint Forces Staff College, Norfolk, Va.
2008 Leadership Enhancement Program, Center for Creative Leadership, Greensboro, N.C.
2008 Air Force Enterprise Leadership Seminar, Kenan-Flagler Business School, University of North Carolina, Chapel Hill, N.C.
2011 Black Sea Security Program, Kennedy School of Government, Harvard University, Cambridge, Mass.
2011 Joint Force Air Component Commander Course, Air University, Maxwell AFB, Ala.
2012 Political-Economic Conflict Seminar, Middle East, Washington, D.C.
2012 Cyber Operations Executive Course, Air University, Maxwell AFB, Ala.
2013 Joint Flag Officer Warfighting Course, Maxwell AFB, Ala

ASSIGNMENTS
1. August 1983 - April 1986, Chief Satellite Officer and Evaluator, NORAD Cheyenne Mountain Complex, Colo.
2. April 1986 - April 1988, Chief, Operations Development Branch, Air Force Space Command, Peterson AFB, Colo.
3. April 1988 - May 1991, Staff Officer and Executive Officer, National Reconnaissance Office, Washington, D.C.
4. May 1991 - March 1993, Section Chief and Titan IV Launch Controller, Cape Canaveral Air Force Station, Fla.
5. March 1993 - June 1994, Deputy, Standardization and Evaluation and Chief, Current Operations, Patrick AFB, Fla.
6. June 1994 - July 1995, Student, U.S. Army Command and General Staff College, Fort Leavenworth, Kan.
7. July 1995 - July 1996, Chief, Space Policy, Office of the Assistant Secretary of the Air Force, Washington, D.C.
8. July 1996 - March 1998, Chief, Space and Missile Branch, Office of Legislative Liaison, Washington, D.C.
9. March 1998 - June 2000, Commander, 2nd Space Operations Squadron, Schriever AFB, Colo.

10. June 2000 - July 2000, Deputy, Commander's Action Group, Air Force Space Command, Peterson AFB, Colo.
11. July 2000 - March 2001, Professional Staff Member, Commission to Assess National Security Space Management and Organization, Washington, D.C.
12. March 2001 - July 2001, Special Assistant to the Deputy Secretary of Defense for Space Commission Implementation, Office of the Secretary of Defense, Washington, D.C.
13. July 2001 - June 2002, National Defense Fellow, Center for Strategic and International Studies, Washington, D.C.
14. June 2002 - July 2003, Senior Adviser, Space, Intelligence, and C4ISR, Office of Secretary of Defense, Washington, D.C.
15. July 2003 - June 2004, Director, Planning and Preparation, Office of Secretary of Defense, Washington, D.C.
16. June 2004 - June 2006, Commander, 50th Operations Group, Schriever AFB, Colo. (October 2005 - February 2006, Director of Space Forces, U.S. Central Command Air Forces, Southwest Asia)
17. June 2006 - September 2006, Vice Commander, 460th Space Wing, Buckley AFB, Colo.
18. September 2006 - April 2008, Commander, Space Development and Test Wing, Kirtland AFB, N.M.
19. May 2007 - April 2008, Director, Joint Operationally Responsive Space Office, Kirtland AFB, N.M.
20. April 2008 - July 2010, Vice Commander, U.S. Air Force Warfare Center, Nellis AFB, Nev.
21. July 2010 - February 2012, Deputy Director, Global Operations (DJ3), U.S. Strategic Command, Offutt AFB, Neb.
22. February 2012 – June 2013, Director, Space Operations, Headquarters U.S. Air Force, Washington, D.C.
23. June 2013- July 2014, Commander, 24th Air Force and Commander, Air Forces Cyber, Joint Base San Antonio - Lackland, Texas
24. August 2014 – present, Deputy Commander, U.S. Cyber Command, Fort Meade, Md.

SUMMARY OF JOINT ASSIGNMENTS
1. August 1983 - April 1986, Chief Satellite Officer and Chief Satellite Officer evaluator, Space Defense Operations Center, Headquarters U.S. Space Command, NORAD Cheyenne Mountain Complex, Colo., as lieutenant
2. April 1988 - May 1991, Deputy for Joint Operations, Executive Officer to the Deputy Director, and Deputy for Space Policy, National Reconnaissance Office, Washington, D.C., as a captain
3. July 2000 - March 2001, Professional Staff Member, Commission to Assess National Security Space Management and Organization, Washington, D.C., as a lieutenant colonel
4. March 2001 - July 2001, Special Assistant to the Deputy Secretary of Defense for Space Commission Implementation, Office of the Secretary of Defense, Washington, D.C., as a lieutenant colonel
5. June 2002 - July 2003, Senior Adviser for Space, Intelligence and C4ISR, Office of the Under Secretary of Defense for Policy, Washington, D.C., as a lieutenant colonel
6. July 2003 - June 2004, Director, Planning and Preparation, Office of the Under Secretary of Defense for Intelligence, Washington, D.C., as a colonel
7. May 2007 - April 2008, Director, Joint Operationally Responsive Space Office, Kirtland AFB, N.M., as a colonel
8. July 2010 - February 2012, Deputy Director, Global Operations (DJ3), U.S. Strategic Command, Offutt AFB, Neb., as a brigadier general
9. August 2014 – present, Deputy Commander, U.S. Cyber Command, Fort Meade, Md.

MAJOR AWARDS AND DECORATIONS
Defense Superior Service Medal with two oak leaf clusters
Legion of Merit with two oak leaf clusters
Defense Meritorious Service Medal with oak leaf cluster
Meritorious Service Medal with two oak leaf clusters
Joint Service Commendation Medal

Air Force Achievement Medal
Humanitarian Service Medal

OTHER ACHIEVEMENTS
2012 General Jerome F. O'Malley Distinguished Space Leadership Award

EFFECTIVE DATES OF PROMOTION
Second Lieutenant June 1, 1983
First Lieutenant June 1, 1985
Captain June 1, 1987
Major March 1, 1994
Lieutenant Colonel Sept. 1, 1998
Colonel July 1, 2003
Brigadier General Dec. 9, 2008
Major General July 3, 2012
Lieutenant General Aug. 4, 2014

(Current as of August 2014)

Brigadier General Charles L. Moore, Jr.
Joint Chiefs of Staff, J-39

Brig. Gen. Charles L. Moore, Jr. is the Deputy Director, Global Operations (J-39). He serves as the Joint Staff focal point for information operations, military information support operations, cyber operations, electronic warfare, special technical operations, and sensitive DOD support to government agencies.

General Moore was commissioned in 1989 after graduating from the U.S. Air Force Academy. He has served as an F-16 fighter pilot, instructor pilot, weapons officer, forward air controller, and instructor at the U.S. Air Force Fighter Weapons School, Nellis AFB, Nev. His command experience includes: the 555th Fighter Squadron at Aviano Air Base Italy, the 332nd Expeditionary Operations Group at Balad AB Iraq, the 20th Fighter Wing at Shaw AFB, S.C. and the 57th Wing at Nellis AFB Nev.

General Moore is a command pilot with more than 3,000 hours in the F-16 and more than 640 hours of combat time

EDUCATION
1989 Bachelor of Science, U.S. Air Force Academy, Colo.
1995 Squadron Officer School, Maxwell AFB, Ala.
1999 Masters of Human Resource Management, Troy State University
2002 Masters of Military Operational Art/Science, Air Command and Staff College, Maxwell AFB, Ala.
2004 Air War College, by correspondence
2006 Air Force National Defense Fellow, Weatherhead Center for International Affairs, Harvard University
2011 Executive Leadership Seminar, Darden School of Business, University of Virginia
2012 Joint Forces Air Component Commander Course, Maxwell AFB, Ala.
2013 Executive Space Operations Course, Nellis AFB, Nev.

ASSIGNMENTS
1. November 1989 - March 1991, Student, Undergraduate Euro-NATO Joint Jet Pilot Training, Sheppard AFB, Texas
2. April 1991 - October 1991, Student, F-16 Replacement Training Unit, 314th Fighter Squadron, Luke AFB, Ariz.
3. October 1991 - August 1992, F-16 Pilot, Assistant Weapons Officer, 314th FS, Luke AFB, Ariz.
4. September 1992 - January 1994, F-16 Pilot, 78th Fighter Squadron, Shaw AFB, S.C.
5. January 1994 - January 1997, F-16 Instructor Pilot, Wing Electronic Combat Pilot, 20th Operations Group, Shaw AFB, S.C.
6. January 1997 - February 1998, F-16 Pilot and Weapons Officer, 35th Fighter Squadron, Kunsan AB, South Korea
7. February 1998 - August 2001, F-16 Instructor Pilot, Assistant Operations Officer, U.S. Air Force Weapons School, Nellis AFB, Nev.
8. June 2002 - June 2004, F-35/JSF Program Capabilities and Requirements Manager, Headquarters AF/XORC
9. June 2004 - July 2006, F-16 Pilot, Operations Officer, and Commander, 555th Fighter Squadron, Aviano AB, Italy
10. June 2007 - June 2008, Commander, 332nd Expeditionary Operations Group, Balad AB, Iraq
11. July 2008 - June 2010, Headquarters NORAD Vice Director of Operations, Peterson AFB, Colo.
12. June 2010 - March 2012, Commander, 20th Fighter Wing, Shaw AFB, S.C.
13. April 2012 - March 2014, Commander, 57th Wing, Nellis AFB, NV
14. March 2014 - July 2014, Chief of Security Assistance, Office of Security Cooperation-Iraq, Baghdad, Iraq

15. July 2014 - March 2015, Deputy Chief, Office of Security Cooperation-Iraq, Baghdad, Iraq
16. March 2015 - present, Deputy Director, Global Operations (J39), J-3, the Joint Staff, the Pentagon, Washington, D.C.

SUMMARY OF JOINT ASSIGNMENTS
1. July 2008 - June 2010, Headquarters NORAD Vice Director of Operations, Peterson AFB, Colo., as a colonel
2. March 2014 - present, Chief of Security Assistance and Deputy Chief, Office of Security Cooperation – Iraq, U.S. Embassy, Baghdad, Iraq, as a brigadier general
3. March 2015 - present, Deputy Director, Global Operations (J39), J-3, the Joint Staff, the Pentagon, Washington, D.C., as a brigadier general

FLIGHT INFORMATION
Rating: command pilot
Flight hours: more than 3,000
Aircraft flown: T-37, T-38, AT-38, F-16 Blocks 30/40/50, F-15C, F-15E, F-18, B-1, B-52, HH-60, MQ-1, MQ-9

MAJOR AWARDS AND DECORATIONS
Defense Superior Service Medal with oak leaf cluster
Bronze Star
Legion of Merit with one oak leaf cluster
Meritorious Service Medal with three oak leaf clusters
Air Medal with seven oak leaf clusters
Aerial Achievement Medal with two oak leaf clusters
Air Force Commendation Medal
Air Force Achievement Medal
Joint Meritorious Unit Award with Gold Border
Meritorious Unit Award
Air Force Outstanding Unit Award with three oak leaf clusters
Air Force Organizational Excellence Award
Combat Readiness Medal
National Defense Service Medal with bronze star
Southwest Asia Service Medal with bronze star
Afghanistan Campaign Medal with bronze star
Iraq Campaign Medal with two bronze stars
Global War on Terrorism Service Medal
Korean Defense Service Medal

OTHER ACHIEVEMENTS
1990 Distinguished graduate, Undergraduate Pilot Training
1991 Distinguished graduate, F-16 RTU
1995 Distinguished graduate, Squadron Officer School
1996 Distinguished graduate/outstanding graduate, U.S. Air Force Weapons School
2005 Commander, USAFE Fighter Squadron of the Year
2007 Clarence H. Mackay Trophy

EFFECTIVE DATES OF PROMOTION
Second Lieutenant May 31, 1989
First Lieutenant May 31, 1991
Captain May 31, 1993
Major April 1, 1998
Lieutenant Colonel March 1, 2003
Colonel Jan. 1, 2007
Brigadier General Nov. 2, 2012   (Current as of April 2015)

WITNESS RESPONSES TO QUESTIONS ASKED DURING THE HEARING

JUNE 22, 2016

RESPONSE TO QUESTION SUBMITTED BY MR. THORNBERRY

Mr. ATKIN. At the NATO Summit in Wales in 2014, Allies affirmed that cyber defense is a key part of NATO's core task of collective defense and agreed that a cyberattack could reach the threshold of an armed attack which could potentially trigger an Article 5 (i.e., collective self-defense) response.

NATO did not specify the threshold at which a cyberattack might constitute an armed attack. Similar to kinetic attack, a cyberattack and its effects would be assessed on a case-by-case and fact-specific basis by the victim nation. If the victim nation decided that an attack were an armed attack, it could then submit a request to the North Atlantic Council for an Article 5 response.

NATO's lack of specificity regarding the threshold for a cyberattack is consistent with U.S. policy. When determining whether a cyber incident constitutes an armed attack, the U.S. Government considers a number of factors including the nature and extent of injury or death to persons and the destruction of, or damage to, property. Besides effects, other factors may also be relevant to a determination, including the context of the event, the identity of the actor perpetrating the action, the target and its location, and the intent of the actor, among other factors. [See page 25.]

RESPONSES TO QUESTIONS SUBMITTED BY MR. ROGERS

Mr. ATKIN. DOD does not "blacklist" suppliers or individual products. It does create Approved Product or Supplier Lists (Whitelists) of products or organizations that have been assessed for use in certain applications. There are currently no Huawei or ZTE products on the DOD Unified Capabilities Approved Products List (APL). The fact that a product does not appear on an APL does not mean contractors cannot offer bids or that the government can still select outside the APL. Short of suspension and debarment, federal contractors and vendors are not precluded from competing on DOD contracts. It is the policy of the DOD to solicit from a broad number of potential offerors and award contracts based on full and open competition to the maximum extent possible.

ZTE Corporation is a unique case because the Department of Commerce added it to the Entity List, which is a list of foreign entities that are subject to specific license requirements for the export, reexport, or transfer of items subject to the Export Administration Regulations. [See page 22.]

General MCLAUGHLIN. [The information referred to is classified and retained in the committee files.] [See page 22.]

RESPONSE TO QUESTION SUBMITTED BY MR. ASHFORD

Mr. ATKIN. The ITEP program is the only IT/Cybersecurity-specific personnel exchange program currently available to the Department. At the end of 2015, DOD–CIO established a management office to oversee the ITEP program and identified a funding source. The program office has been able to identify, vet, and place three industry participants in DOD positions and five DOD Civilian personnel in industry positions. The program office is working to vet additional candidates and place another two candidates to meet program capacity allotted in the ITEP legislation. [See page 20.]

QUESTIONS SUBMITTED BY MEMBERS POST HEARING

JUNE 22, 2016

QUESTIONS SUBMITTED BY MR. ROGERS

Mr. ROGERS. Do you recommend the Department of Defense rely on equipment provided by Huawei or ZTE, which are linked to the Chinese military and intelligence apparatus and have been linked to sales to the Islamic Republic of Iran, in violation of U.S. sanctions laws?

Mr. ATKIN. DOD does not "blacklist" suppliers or individual products. It does create Approved Product or Supplier Lists (Whitelists) of products or organizations that have been assessed for use in certain applications. There are currently no Huawei or ZTE products on the DOD Unified Capabilities Approved Products List (APL). The fact that a product does not appear on an APL does not mean contractors cannot offer bids or that the government can still select outside the APL. Short of suspension and debarment, federal contractors and vendors are not precluded from competing on DOD contracts. It is the policy of the DOD to solicit from a broad number of potential offerors and award contracts based on full and open competition to the maximum extent possible.

ZTE Corporation is a unique case because the Department of Commerce added it to the Entity List, which is a list of foreign entities that are subject to specific license requirements for the export, reexport, or transfer of items subject to the Export Administration Regulations.

Mr. ROGERS. If a U.S. cleared defense contractor came to you and stated that they were planning to buy IT equipment or network management services from Huawei or ZTE, what would you advise them? What are the risks of using such equipment or network management services?

Mr. ATKIN. In addition to advising the cleared defense contractor that they should conduct commercial due diligence of the provider of equipment or services, we would recommend they practice supply chain risk management best practices such as those in the National Institute of Science and Technology Special Publication 800–161, "Supply Chain Risk Management Practices for Federal Information Systems and Organizations." If the equipment or services were for use on or related to a national security system, DOD would also reference the policies and procedures in Committee on National Security Systems Directive 505, "Supply Chain Risk Management," and DOD Instruction 5200.44, "Protection of Mission Critical Functions to Achieve Trusted Systems and Networks (TSN)."

Only in limited circumstances would the Department have insight into or the contractual right to control a cleared defense contractor's decision to use any particular subcontractor or supplier. Absent suspension or debarment or a statutory restriction on contracting with a prohibited source, our cleared defense contractors would generally not be precluded from using a specific vendor's equipment or services.

However, it is important to note that the Department has several mechanisms in place to help ensure the security of products or services delivered to us and the systems that cleared defense contractors use to store or process sensitive DOD information.

First, the Department requires Program Protection Plans (PPPs) to address the full spectrum of security risks for the critical components contained in our weapons systems, including supply chain vulnerabilities, and to implement mitigations to manage risk to system functionality. In addition to the security requirements applied to deliverable products or services, the Federal Acquisition Regulation (FAR) requires that contractor information systems used to store or process classified information are compliant with the National Industrial Security Program Operating Manual (NISPOM). The Defense FAR Supplement (DFARS) also requires that contractor unclassified systems that will store or process sensitive DOD information must also provide appropriate security for that information.

It is important to note that there are additional statutory authorities available to the Department to limit or exclude vendors in specific circumstances. For example, section 1211 of the National Defense Authorization Act (NDAA) for Fiscal Year (FY) 2006, as amended by section 1243 of the NDAA for FY 2012, and as implemented at DFARS Section 225.77, prohibits the Secretary of Defense from acquiring supplies or services that are on the United States Munitions List through a contract, or subcontract at any tier, from any Communist Chinese military company. In addition, section 806 of the NDAA for FY 2011, as amended by section 806 of the NDAA for FY 2013, has been implemented at DFARS Subpart 239.73, "Requirements for Information Relating to Supply Chain Risk." This clause enables DOD components to exclude a source that fails to meet established qualifications standards or fails to receive an acceptable rating for an evaluation factor regarding supply chain risk for information technology acquisitions, and to withhold consent for a contractor to subcontract with a particular source or to direct a contractor to exclude a particular source.

ZTE Corporation is a unique case because the Department of Commerce added it to the Entity List, which is a list of foreign entities that are subject to specific license requirements for the export, reexport, or transfer of items subject to the Export Administration Regulations.

Mr. ROGERS. What if that same cleared defense contractor told you that because of their relationship with Huawei, they were being asked or were required to submit information related to their network security? What would you suggest they do? What are the risks of providing information about their network security to a firm like Huawei?

Mr. ATKIN. DOD would advise the cleared defense contractor that they should conduct commercial due diligence of the provider of equipment or services they partner with. For the specific example of providing network security information to a company in which they outsource services, DOD would additionally advise the cleared defense contractor to conduct a risk analysis based on the type of information, what type of access to the information is provided (can information be modified), contractual provisions on how the information will be used or shared, and information protections, among other factors.

Mr. ROGERS. Do you recommend the Department of Defense rely on equipment provided by Huawei or ZTE, which are linked to the Chinese military and intelligence apparatus and have been linked to sales to the Islamic Republic of Iran, in violation of U.S. sanctions laws?

General McLAUGHLIN. [The information referred to is classified and retained in the committee files.]

Mr. ROGERS. If a U.S. cleared defense contractor came to you and stated that they were planning to buy IT equipment or network management services from Huawei or ZTE, what would you advise them? What are the risks of using such equipment or network management services?

General McLAUGHLIN. [The information referred to is classified and retained in the committee files.]

Mr. ROGERS. What if that same cleared defense contractor told you that because of their relationship with Huawei, they were being asked or were required to submit information related to their network security? What would you suggest they do? What are the risks of providing information about their network security to a firm like Huawei?

General McLAUGHLIN. [The information referred to is classified and retained in the committee files.]

Mr. ROGERS. Do you recommend the Department of Defense rely on equipment provided by Huawei or ZTE, which are linked to the Chinese military and intelligence apparatus and have been linked to sales to the Islamic Republic of Iran, in violation of U.S. sanctions laws?

General MOORE. [The information referred to is classified and retained in the committee files.]

Mr. ROGERS. If a U.S. cleared defense contractor came to you and stated that they were planning to buy IT equipment or network management services from Huawei or ZTE, what would you advise them? What are the risks of using such equipment or network management services?

General MOORE. [The information referred to is classified and retained in the committee files.]

Mr. ROGERS. What if that same cleared defense contractor told you that because of their relationship with Huawei, they were being asked or were required to submit information related to their network security? What would you suggest they do? What are the risks of providing information about their network security to a firm like Huawei?

General MOORE. [The information referred to is classified and retained in the committee files.]

QUESTIONS SUBMITTED BY MR. LAMBORN

Mr. LAMBORN. Regarding Sec. 1107 of FY16 NDAA, the authority to create a Title 10 Civilian Cyber Excepted Service Workforce: Since cyberspace is a warfighting domain, are these civilian personnel lawful combatants? Should they be? If they are, are we willing to accept that in a multi-domain military conflict that they could be targeted by our adversaries no differently than our uniformed personnel?

Mr. ATKIN. The great majority of the activities envisioned for our DOD civilian cyber workforce are support activities, such as, by way of example, developing information technology strategy and designing computer systems required to support an enterprise's objectives and goals, conducting routine network maintenance and security functions, developing offensive and defensive tools and capabilities, and providing technical advice or services to members of the armed forces and to departmental chief information officers. Notably, the great majority of the activities envisioned for our DOD civilian workforce are conducted during peacetime, when their role in hostilities is not in question.

During armed conflict, under the law of war, persons who are not members of the U.S. armed forces, but are authorized to accompany them, fall into a special category. Although they are often referred to as "civilians" because they are not military personnel, they differ materially from the civilian population because these persons are sometimes also authorized—and in some cases, are ordered—to accompany U.S. armed forces into a theater of operations to support the force. Persons authorized to accompany the U.S. armed forces may not be made the object of attack un- less they take direct part in hostilities. They may, however, be detained by enemy military forces, and are entitled to POW status if they fall into the power of the enemy during international armed conflict. They also have legal immunity from the enemy's domestic law for providing authorized support services to the armed forces. However, during armed conflict, some civilians who support the U.S. armed forces may sit at the keyboard and participate, under the direction of a military com- mander, in cyberspace operations. The law of war does not prohibit civilians from directly participating in hostilities, such as offensive or defensive cyberspace oper- ations, even when that activity would be a use of force or would involve direct par- ticipation in hostilities; however, in such cases, a civilian is not a "lawful combat- ant" and does not enjoy the right of combatant immunity, is subject to direct attack for such time as he or she directly participates in hostilities, and if captured by enemy government forces may be prosecuted for acts prohibited under the captor's domestic law.

Most, if not the great majority, of our civilian cyber workforce involved in providing support to cyberspace operations during armed conflict will not be serving on the battlefield where they may be the object of attack or risk being detained by the enemy. Instead, most will be providing their support remotely from areas outside the area of hostilities, are not easily identifiable as an individual, and are likely serving in the United States. DOD practice has been to permit a broad range of civilians to be authorized to accompany U.S. armed forces, such as, by way of example, DOD employees, employees of other government agencies sent to support the U.S. armed forces, and other authorized persons working on government contracts to support the U.S. armed forces. The DOD civilian cyber workforce is another cat- egory of DOD employees who may support the armed forces on the battlefield and elsewhere. DOD expects its commanders to exercise care in placing any civilian ac- companying U.S. armed forces in situations in which an attacking enemy may con- sider their activities to constitute taking a direct part in hostilities. It would be an exceptional situation where any member of the DOD civilian cyber work force would be subject to any greater risk than other civilians accompanying the armed forces.

Mr. LAMBORN. Regarding Sec. 1107 of FY16 NDAA, the authority to create a Title 10 Civilian Cyber Excepted Service Workforce: Acknowledging that civilians are vital to our cyberspace activities, were the Sec. 1107 authorities sufficient, or are others needed?

Mr. ATKIN. The Section 1107 authorities provide the Department with new capa- bilities to improve recruiting and retention of cyber personnel that DOD is in the very initial stages of implementing. In our view, there is a potential issue with the scope of the authority. It appears somewhat limited, depending on its interpretation. A broader and more clearly defined scope that includes positions held by elements of the Department of Defense supporting the Department's cyberspace mission would be helpful as well as authorities that provide enhanced recruiting, training, professional development, and retention capabilities to the Secretary of Defense through a centralized Cyber Workforce Development Fund. The authorities in title 10 provided to the Secretary for a similar fund, the Department of Defense Acquisi- tion Workforce Development Fund, dedicated to the development and sustainment of the defense acquisition workforce and managed by the Under Secretary of Defense for Acquisition, Technology and Logistics, provide a useful model.

———

QUESTIONS SUBMITTED BY MR. O'ROURKE

Mr. O'ROURKE. 1) How large is the CYBERCOM workforce? Please break down by civilian, Active Duty, and contractor.

2) How is DOD competing with the private sector to get high-quality talent to fill cyber security positions? Do you anticipate DOD becoming more dependent on the contracted workforce for this purpose? How do our potential adversaries deal with this problem?

Mr. ATKIN. NDAA FY16, Sec 1107 will improve DOD's competitive posture for cyber talent. The Department will use this new authority to address hiring challenges by establishing a new DOD Cyber Excepted Service. Using a phased approach, the Department will implement the new personnel system for United States Cyber Command and supporting organizations to recruit and retain highly skilled cyber personnel. It is too soon to tell whether the Department will become more dependent on the contracted workforce at this time.

Mr. O'ROURKE. 1) How large is the CYBERCOM workforce? Please break down by civilian, Active Duty, and contractor.

2) How is DOD competing with the private sector to get high-quality talent to fill cyber security positions? Do you anticipate DOD becoming more dependent on the contracted workforce for this purpose? How do our potential adversaries deal with this problem?

General McLAUGHLIN. [The information referred to is for official use only and retained in the committee files.]

Mr. O'ROURKE. 1) How large is the CYBERCOM workforce? Please break down by civilian, Active Duty, and contractor.

2) How is DOD competing with the private sector to get high-quality talent to fill cyber security positions? Do you anticipate DOD becoming more dependent on the contracted workforce for this purpose? How do our potential adversaries deal with this problem?

General MOORE. [The information referred to is classified and retained in the committee files.]

———

QUESTIONS SUBMITTED BY MR. AGUILAR

Mr. AGUILAR. In the testimony presented, you mentioned the "Cybersecurity National Action Plan" released by the President. One of the proposals mentioned in the plan was "enhancing student loan forgiveness programs for Cybersecurity experts joining the Federal workforce." You mention the "need to keep our best employees," in your testimony. From what you have seen, do you believe enhanced student loan forgiveness would assist us in retaining the best personnel? Why? Also, do you know of any current efforts to implement any enhanced loan forgiveness programs within the DOD?

Mr. ATKIN. Given the significant rise in the cost of higher education, as well as the number of students who graduate with a student loan burden, this could be an attractive recruiting tool to get young, highly talented cybersecurity personnel into the Federal Government and develop them as long term employees. Its usefulness as a retention tool for individuals already in federal service is unknown, without knowing the details of the program. An enhanced loan forgiveness program within DOD would likely require a legislative proposal.

Mr. AGUILAR. In our efforts to identify, recruit, and retain qualified cyber operations personnel, what would you all say, each of you, are the three biggest obstacles?

Mr. ATKIN. The three biggest obstacles are: 1) Cyber operations is a high demand skill area across the federal government, private sector, etc., creating significant competition across all sectors for experienced personnel. 2) DOD does not provide competitive salaries, although the new Section 1107 authorities will help in that regard. 3) The lack of a Cyber Workforce Development Fund that mirrors the Defense Acquisition Workforce Development Fund (CWDF). The CWDF would strongly support the Department's efforts to recruit, train and develop a system to carefully manage our civilian cyber workforce.

Mr. AGUILAR. You mention in your testimony that "one of the Department's key policy goals in cyberspace is to deter cyberattacks." And while I agree that such a goal is a worthy endeavor, one of the attributes of other weapons is that they have a clearly defined "home address." We can tell where a missile is shot from. Cyberattacks, however, are far more ambiguous and real questions exist about the ability to accurately trace the source of an attack. I understand the limits of what can be discussed in such an open forum, but could you all speak a little to the steps we are taking to improve our ability to correctly attribute attacks to actors?

Mr. ATKIN. Attribution is a fundamental part of an effective cyber deterrence strategy, as anonymity enables malicious cyber activity by state and non-state groups. Intelligence and attribution capabilities help unmask an actor's cyber persona, identify the attack's point of origin, and determine tactics, techniques, and procedures. Public or private attribution can play a significant role in dissuading cyber actors from conducting attacks in the first place. Attribution also enables the Defense Department or other agencies to conduct response and denial operations against an incoming cyberattack, and ensure that any response targets the responsible actor and is discriminate and proportional and in accordance with international and domestic law—just as we do in any domain.

This is why DOD and the intelligence community have invested significantly in all source collection, analysis, and dissemination capabilities, all of which reduce the anonymity of state and non-state actor activity in cyberspace. DOD is also collaborating with the private sector and other agencies of the U.S. government to strengthen attribution capabilities.

Mr. AGUILAR. In the testimony presented, you mentioned the "Cybersecurity National Action Plan" released by the President. One of the proposals mentioned in the plan was "enhancing student loan forgiveness programs for Cybersecurity experts joining the Federal workforce." You mention the "need to keep our best employees," in your testimony. From what you have seen, do you believe enhanced student loan forgiveness would assist us in retaining the best personnel? Why? Also, do you know of any current efforts to implement any enhanced loan forgiveness programs within the DOD?

General MCLAUGHLIN. The fight for cyber talent requires a full arsenal of hiring flexibilities. Benefits like loan forgiveness give hiring managers and additional tool to entice potential new hires. Beyond the Secretary of Defense's direction to delegate approval authority for hiring flexibilities (such as loan forgiveness) to the service cyber component commanders, I am unaware of any additional effort to expand loan forgiveness throughout the department.

Mr. AGUILAR. In our efforts to identify, recruit, and retain qualified cyber operations personnel, what would you all say, each of you, are the three biggest obstacles?

General MCLAUGHLIN. We believe competition, lack of professionalization (not to be confused with professionalism) and operations tempo are the biggest obstacles to identifying, recruiting and retaining qualified cyber operations personnel.
Competition:
Highly qualified cyber professionals continue to be in high demand, but low quantity. Many candidates simple don't have the patience to wait on the lengthy federal hiring process, which includes gaining security clearances; nor do they have the desire to accept lower wages set by federal compensation rules. New personnel often wait many months prior to starting, even after completing training and reporting to their duty stations. Many of the young qualified people we are recruiting are also being targeted by colleges and private industry that provide many other competitive opportunities, often paying more money. Additionally, once many of our military have served their initial term, they have received high-quality training that makes them desirable to the private sector, causing many of them to consider leaving the services.
Professionalization:
A "cyber warrior" can be molded from a host of different career fields. From on-net operators, to linguists and operational planners, cyber professional' career paths are intermingled with other professional specialties. Unlike the intelligence or special operations community, cyber does not have a well-worn path to career advancement. As such, many in our community feel isolated and have difficulty seeing advancement within what could be a lifelong profession.
Operations Tempo:
The cyber domain is growing exponentially, and it has quickly out-paced the department's ability to match manpower to mission. The workforce at every echelon, across occupational specialties, is tasked to [the] hilt, and task saturation is compounding the issue of retention.

Mr. AGUILAR. You mention in your testimony that "one of the Department's key policy goals in cyberspace is to deter cyberattacks." And while I agree that such a goal is a worthy endeavor, one of the attributes of other weapons is that they have a clearly defined "home address." We can tell where a missile is shot from. Cyberattacks however, are far more ambiguous and real questions exist about the ability to accurately trace the source of an attack. I understand the limits of what can be discussed in such an open forum, but could you all speak a little to the steps we are taking to improve our ability to correctly attribute attacks to actors?

General McLAUGHLIN. Attribution is a fundamental part of an effective cyber deterrence strategy, as anonymity enables malicious cyber activity by state and non-state groups. Intelligence and attribution capabilities help unmask an actor's cyber persona, identify the attack's point of origin, and determine tactics, techniques, and procedures. Public or private attribution can play a significant role in dissuading cyber actors from conducting attacks in the first place. Attribution also enables the Defense Department or other agencies to conduct response and denial operations against an incoming cyberattack, and ensure that any response targets the responsible actor and is discriminate and proportional and in accordance with international and domestic law—just as we do in any domain.

This is why DOD and the intelligence community have invested significantly in all source collection, analysis, and dissemination capabilities, all of which reduce the anonymity of state and non-state actor activity in cyberspace. DOD is also collaborating with the private sector and other agencies of the U.S. government to strengthen attribution capabilities.

Mr. AGUILAR. In the testimony presented, you mentioned the "Cybersecurity National Action Plan" released by the President. One of the proposals mentioned in the plan was "enhancing student loan forgiveness programs for Cybersecurity experts joining the Federal workforce." You mention the "need to keep our best employees," in your testimony. From what you have seen, do you believe enhanced student loan forgiveness would assist us in retaining the best personnel? Why? Also, do you know of any current efforts to implement any enhanced loan forgiveness programs within the DOD?

General MOORE. Given the significant rise in the cost of higher education, as well as the number of students who graduate with a student loan burden, this could be an attractive recruiting tool to get young, highly talented cybersecurity personnel into the Federal Government and develop them as long term employees. Its usefulness as a retention tool for individuals already in federal service is unknown, without knowing the details of the program. An enhanced loan forgiveness program within DOD would likely require a legislative proposal. There is no effort in progress of which we are aware.

Mr. AGUILAR. In our efforts to identify, recruit, and retain qualified cyber operations personnel, what would you all say, each of you, are the three biggest obstacles?

General MOORE. 1. Compensation disparity. DOD is hard pressed to compete with the private sector in terms of salaries for highly qualified cyber operations personnel. For both DOD civilians as well as military service members, private companies and corporations offer significantly higher salaries for the same level of expertise. This exacerbates the problem of recruiting and retaining individuals with these skills within the DOD.

2. Also, compounding the problem further is the fact that the more training and experience the DOD provides to its employees, the more marketable they become and the greater the gap between their military or GS-civilian pay and the corresponding private sector pay.

3. Supply vs. Demand. Within the United States there is currently a gap between the demand for qualified cyber operations and security personnel, and the supply of workers with these skills. The U.S. simply does not have enough graduates in STEM and Computer Science fields to meet the booming demand from both the public and private sectors. In competing for this scarce resource of human capital, the DOD is up against not only Silicon Valley companies such as Apple, Facebook, and Alphabet, but also large corporations across many other sectors of the economy, as well as other federal and state government agencies.

Mr. AGUILAR. You mention in your testimony that "one of the Department's key policy goals in cyberspace is to deter cyberattacks." And while I agree that such a goal is a worthy endeavor, one of the attributes of other weapons is that they have a clearly defined "home address." We can tell where a missile is shot from. Cyberattacks however, are far more ambiguous and real questions exist about the ability to accurately trace the source of an attack. I understand the limits of what can be discussed in such an open forum, but could you all speak a little to the steps we are taking to improve our ability to correctly attribute attacks to actors?

General MOORE. Attribution is a fundamental part of an effective cyber deterrence strategy, as anonymity enables malicious cyber activity by state and non-state groups. Intelligence and attribution capabilities help unmask an actor's cyber persona, identify the attack's point of origin, and determine tactics, techniques, and procedures. Public or private attribution can play a significant role in dissuading cyber actors from conducting attacks in the first place. Attribution also enables the Defense Department or other agencies to conduct response and denial operations against an incoming cyberattack, and ensure that any response targets the responsible actor and is discriminate and proportional and in accordance with international and domestic law—just as we do in any domain.

This is why DOD and the intelligence community have invested significantly in all source collection, analysis, and dissemination capabilities, all of which reduce the anonymity of state and non-state actor activity in cyberspace. DOD is also collaborating with the private sector and other agencies of the U.S. government to strengthen attribution capabilities.